Don't ever let a recipe tell you how many chocolate chips to use. You measure that with your heart.

THE
CHOCOLATE
CHIP COOKIE
BOOK

CLASSIC, CREATIVE, AND MUST-TRY RECIPES FOR EVERY KITCHEN

KATIE JACOBS

Join the Chocolate Chip Cookie Club
at thechocolatechipcookiebook.com
for more recipes, video tutorials, and
access to all of Katie's cookie tips.

The Chocolate Chip Cookie Book

Copyright © 2023 Katie Jacobs

Published by Harper Celebrate, an imprint of HarperCollins Focus LLC

All photography by Katie Jacobs, except pages iii, viii, 2, and 130 by Katelyn Brown and pages 4 and 232 by Evin Krehbiel.

Any internet addresses (websites, blogs, etc.) in this book are offered as a resource. They are not intended in any way to be or imply an endorsement by HarperCollins Focus LLC, nor does HarperCollins Focus LLC vouch for the content of these sites for the life of this book.

General Food Safety Disclaimer: The reader assumes full responsibility for using their best judgment when cooking with raw ingredients such as eggs, dairy products, and flour, and seeking information from an official food safety authority if they are unsure. It is the responsibility of the reader to review all listed ingredients in a recipe before cooking to ensure that none of the ingredients may cause a potential adverse reaction to anyone eating the food based on recipes featured. If using a substitution for those recipes labeled vegan, paleo, gluten-free, or dairy-free, please be sure that any substituted ingredient is in line with those dietary restrictions.

ISBN 978-0-7852-9563-1 (ePub)
ISBN 978-0-7852-9562-4 (HC)

Printed in India

24 25 26 27 REP 5 4 3

For Brent, Emmaline,
Joey Kate, and Hunt—
YOU GIVE ME A REASON TO BAKE COOKIES.

CONTENTS

1. THE CLASSICS

2. SPECIALTY COOKIES AND BARS

3. CAKES, PIES, AND GIANT COOKIES

4. THE FUN STUFF

5. HEALTHY(ISH) TREATS

INTRODUCTION

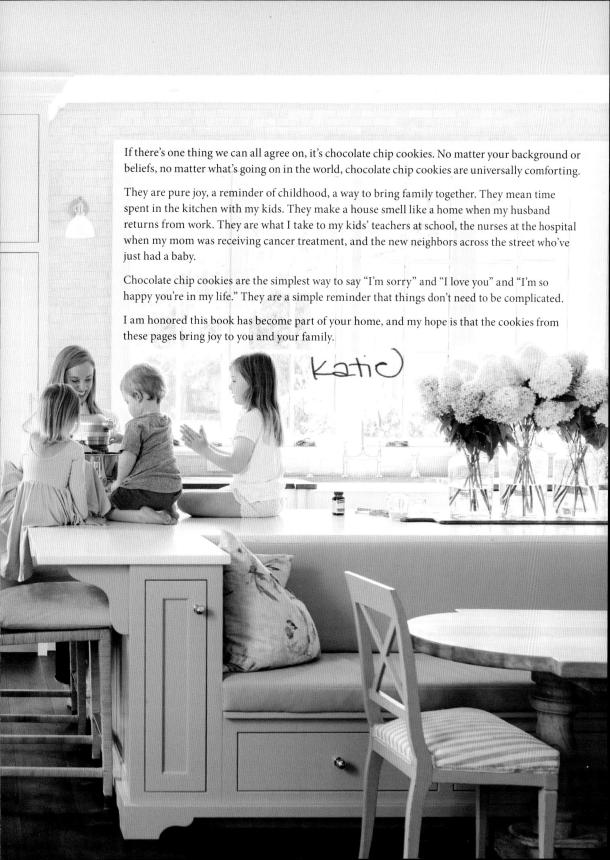

If there's one thing we can all agree on, it's chocolate chip cookies. No matter your background or beliefs, no matter what's going on in the world, chocolate chip cookies are universally comforting.

They are pure joy, a reminder of childhood, a way to bring family together. They mean time spent in the kitchen with my kids. They make a house smell like a home when my husband returns from work. They are what I take to my kids' teachers at school, the nurses at the hospital when my mom was receiving cancer treatment, and the new neighbors across the street who've just had a baby.

Chocolate chip cookies are the simplest way to say "I'm sorry" and "I love you" and "I'm so happy you're in my life." They are a simple reminder that things don't need to be complicated.

I am honored this book has become part of your home, and my hope is that the cookies from these pages bring joy to you and your family.

Katie

HOW TO
USE THIS BOOK?
AS YOU WISH!

This book is laid out in five chapters. We start with the classics because if it ain't broke, don't fix it! Next, we take it beyond the basics with specialty cookies, before blowing the roof off the whole thing with bars, brownies, candies, pies, ice cream, and cakes. There is certainly something for everyone, including recipes for those with food allergies, sensitivities, and dietary restrictions.

I'm excited for you to try the recipes in this book, and my dream is that you will love them and incorporate them into your family's recipe collection. But if you never make a single recipe exactly as written, my hope is that you create a recipe all your own. In the following pages, I'm giving you all the tools you need to go confidently into the kitchen armed with baking knowledge to experiment and have fun. So, for those of you keen on jumping right in, here are some tips and tricks.

KITCHEN TIPS AND TRICKS

STOCK YOUR PANTRY
Chocolate chip cookies all start with the basic ingredients of butter, sugar, brown sugar, eggs, vanilla, flour, baking soda, salt, and chocolate. Always make sure you're well-stocked to bake cookies at a moment's notice. There's nothing worse than getting a craving for cookies only to realize you have to run to the store for flour!

READ THE RECIPE BEFORE YOU BEGIN
Baking will go a lot smoother if you at least skim the recipe before jumping in. Get an idea of how much time something will take and make sure you have the ingredients called for. If you have the time, take it a step further and pre-measure ingredients before starting, making sure everything is in its place (*mise en place*) and ensuring everything will flow smoothly.

LICK THE SPOON
Do this, not just because it's fun, but because it's important to know that things taste right before you put them in the oven.

SET A TIMER
We're all busy. Doing this will make sure you don't burn the cookies!

GET TO MEASURING
Measure ingredients accurately to create an accurate result. In baking, ingredients create chemical reactions that affect rise, texture, and taste. The tiniest change in the measurement of those ingredients can alter the final result. Use a kitchen scale if you need to. I have a conversion chart on page 7 to help.

GET YOUR KIDS IN THE KITCHEN

Baking is supposed to be fun, and letting your kids get in on the fun is a great opportunity for them to spend quality time with you and learn a few things. My three little ones were involved in every recipe in this book. Pull a chair up to the counter so they are at a good height to help. Let them dump measured ingredients into the bowl, and give everyone their own spatula for stirring. Remind them that "we get to taste at the end," and make sure everyone gets a good lick of cookie dough before the cookies go into the oven.

MAKE IT PRETTY

We eat with our eyes first, so while chocolate chip cookies aren't fussy, you still want to make them look pretty! To create a picture-perfect cookie, set aside a handful of the chocolate chips called for in the recipe to place on top of each cookie before baking. When the cookies first come out of the oven, round the sides using a biscuit cutter (see directions in "Tools and Equipment") and add even more chocolate to the tops.

MAKE CLEANUP A BREEZE

Designate a section of your kitchen for baking. Ideally this will be where you keep all your tools and ingredients. That way, everything is within reach and you're not running around making a mess of the entire kitchen. Keep a "trash bowl" on the counter for eggshells, butter wrappers, and anything else that will be thrown away. Use parchment paper or a silicone baking mat on cookie sheets for easy cleanup. When ready for cleanup, throw all the tools that you used into the dirty mixing bowl and set it in the sink. Fill the bowl with *hot* water and let it sit while you clean the counter. When you come back to it, most of the batter will have dissolved in the hot water of the bowl—and washing dishes will now be a breeze.

STORE YOUR COOKIES PROPERLY

Make sure your cookies cool completely before storing. Soft and chewy cookies should be stored at room temperature in an airtight container. Crunchy or crispy cookies should be stored separately from soft cookies in a container with the lid partially unsealed. (The moisture trapped in the container will soften the cookies.)

○○○○○

DIFFICULTY LEVELS AND DIETARY RESTRICTIONS

The recipes in this book are labeled to help gauge level of difficulty (● ○○○○ being the easiest and ● ● ● ● ● being the most difficult). Each recipe is also labeled with the following illustrations for simple at-a-glance reference.

DF = DAIRY-FREE

GF = GLUTEN-FREE

P = PALEO

V = VEGAN

= BROWN BUTTER IS USED

= MIXER IS USED

= ALLOW TIME FOR REFRIGERATION

= ALLOW TIME FOR FREEZING

TOOLS AND EQUIPMENT

Starting with the right equipment makes all the difference. A few clever tools will ensure your prep is simpler, speedier, and more enjoyable.

STAND MIXER
You'll need a stand mixer for most of the recipes in this book. An inexpensive hand mixer will also do the trick. I love a stand mixer because it serves as an extra set of hands, working its magic while you're prepping the next step.

BAKING SHEETS
Always have at least two baking sheets on hand. I recommend flat half-sheet pans (13 x 18-inch). You may also need baking pans or cake pans for some of the recipes in this book.

RUBBER SPATULA AND WHISK
I love using a whisk to combine wet ingredients before switching to a rubber spatula to fold in the dry ingredients. Invest in a heat-resistant spatula for making caramel and brown butter.

OVEN
Conventional ovens take about 10 to 15 minutes to preheat. You never want to place cookie dough in a not-quite-hot-enough oven. If you bake a lot, get an oven thermometer to ensure the best baking results every time.

All the recipes and baking times in this book are configured for a conventional oven. A convection oven has a fan and exhaust system that a regular oven does not have. The fan and exhaust help blow hot oven air over and around the food, then vent it back out. As a result, this hot air surrounds the food so that it cooks evenly and more quickly. If using a convection oven, either reduce the temperature by about 25 degrees or cut the cooking time by 25 percent.

PARCHMENT PAPER AND SILICONE BAKING MATS
I like to buy the pre-cut half sheets of parchment paper, which make it easy to grab and go. I also use a silicone baking mat daily and just wash it in the sink after it has cooled.

BOWLS
You'll need mixing bowls in various sizes. Glass and stainless steel bowls are best for baking.

COOKIE SCOOPS
To achieve uniformly round cookies, use a cookie scoop. I talk about the different size options on page 8.

KITCHEN SCALE

If you're worried about the accuracy of your measurements, a kitchen scale is a great investment. Even ingredients that seem simple to measure, like flour, can vary greatly from person to person. When you weigh the flour for a recipe, you know exactly how much you're using. By contrast, when you measure by volume, the actual amount of flour you use varies based on a variety of factors—your specific measuring cups, how you scoop the flour, how tightly you pack it, and more. If a recipe calls for a cup of flour, you could end up using as much as 1.25 times more. A difference this large can have a huge impact on how your cookies turn out. Here are some helpful conversions.

BAKING CONVERSIONS

These are great to have on hand, especially if you prefer using a kitchen scale.

FLOUR:
1 cup = 4.2 ounces or 120 grams

SUGAR:
1 cup = 7.1 ounces or 200 grams

BROWN SUGAR:
1 cup = 7.8 ounces or 220 grams

BUTTER:
1 cup = 2 sticks or 8 ounces or 225 grams

CHOCOLATE CHIPS:
1 cup = 6 ounces or 170 grams

CONFECTIONERS' SUGAR:
1 cup = 4 ounces or 110 grams

ADDITIONAL EQUIPMENT

These additional tools and equipment are used in the recipes in this book and will be handy for you to have: food processor, blender, aluminum foil, rimmed baking sheets, cooling rack, a candy thermometer, and airtight storage containers.

KNIVES AND CUTTING BOARD

You'll need a serrated knife for chopping chocolate on an anchored cutting board. The serrations on the blade are much better than a chef's knife at "grabbing" the smooth surface of a chocolate bar.

MEASURING CUPS AND SPOONS

Stainless steel cups and spoons are ideal for measuring dry ingredients because they are sturdy and well-balanced. Have several glass measuring cups on hand to measure liquid.

OFFSET SPATULA

Quite possibly my favorite kitchen tool, the offset spatula is perfect for decorating cakes, smoothing out batter, and creating picture-perfect finishing touches.

ROUND COOKIE CUTTER OR BISCUIT CUTTER

This is great for creating perfectly round cookies. When the cookies are hot, just out of the oven, use a round biscuit cutter slightly larger than the cookie to round out the edges of the cookies. Place the cookie cutter around the outside of each cookie and push or swirl the cookie around inside the cutter in a circular motion, gently bating the sides to neaten the edges into a perfect circle.

COOKIE SCOOPS

I specify three different-sized cookie scoops through-out this book: small, medium (what I call regular), and large. The small scoop holds 2 teaspoons of dough and produces a cookie roughly 2 inches in size. The regular, and most common, scoop is a 1.25-ounce scoop (holding $1^{1}/_{2}$ tablespoons of dough), producing a 3-inch cookie. The largest is a 3-tablespoon scoop that gives you a large 4-inch cookie.

A cookie scoop also brings a needed texture to the outside of the cookie dough ball. Scooping and rolling the dough by hand smooths the outside of the cookie dough and creates a smoother cookie top. A cookie scoop creates great ridges and texture.

BAKE TIMES PER SCOOP:

Small: 6 to 8 minutes
Medium: 9 to 10 minutes
Large: 12 to 15 minutes

DOUGH USING A COOKIE SCOOP

DOUGH ROUNDED BY HAND

LARGE SCOOP
3 TBS. OF DOUGH

SMALL SCOOP
2 TSP. OF DOUGH

REGULAR SCOOP
1 1/2 TBS. OF DOUGH

SECRETS AND SCIENCE

CREATING THE PERFECT CHOCOLATE CHIP COOKIE

My mom and my best friend, Elizabeth, and I can all use the exact same chocolate chip cookie recipe, but somehow all of our cookies turn out completely different. For years I couldn't understand it. How could we be using the same recipe and have such different results?

Then I got into the kitchen with my mom. She always has the TV on and twenty-two other things going on. She gets out a large glass bowl and a rubber spatula and tosses in ingredients while asking me, "Did I add the baking soda yet?" She bakes them all at one time on a large, rimmed commercial cookie sheet in her industrial gas oven. She never sets a timer but knows they're done by the smell in her kitchen. She's the originator of the original recipe (the OG of chocolate chip cookies) and makes them by feeling the ingredients more than by measuring—resulting in cookies that look a little different every time she makes them but are always the best cookies I've ever eaten.

I think Elizabeth makes this recipe almost daily— for friends, a church group, or the local police department. She makes them using her KitchenAid mixer and Watkins Vanilla (quite possibly her secret ingredient). She uses a small cookie scoop to get more cookies out of her recipe (which means more to share). Her entire neighborhood, which includes my husband, agrees that her mini cookies, bursting with vanilla flavor, are the best cookies they've ever eaten.

I always have a child on the counter helping me bake. I like to make chocolate chip cookies by hand with the same green rubber spatula that I had in my first apartment, and with my children fighting over who gets to stir. Over the years I've adapted and changed the recipe, experimenting with trends like pan-banging and using brown butter. Usually though, I circle back to the original recipe, changing out the chocolate chips to semi-sweet baking wafers roughly chopped, which creates chocolate layers throughout the cookie. I'll bake cookies for neighbors, include them in dinners for friends who have just had babies, or bring them to Sunday night family dinners. Everyone always raves these are the best cookies they've ever eaten.

All three of us use the exact same recipe, but over the years we have tweaked and changed the original to our own tastes and, dare I say, personality. It got me thinking, when I started writing this book, about how I wanted readers to not only be able to bake the recipes provided but also tweak and change the recipes to suit their evolving palate and create something that embodies their own baking style. I want *you* to be able to bake the best chocolate chip cookies your friends and family have *ever* had.

So, here I've created a grid—a cheat sheet, really—for creating your own perfect cookie. I started with our original recipe, "The Constant," and from there I changed small variables that would alter the outcome of the final product. They're tiny nuances that don't seem to matter when you're stirring ingredients, but this chart helps explain the science behind what each ingredient adds to your batter. If you've ever wondered why a recipe calls for room temperature butter, tells you not to overmix the batter, or makes you refrigerate the dough, this chart will explain it all.

In one day, I baked over 340 cookies to create a chocolate chip cookie road map. Not only did I explore how different ingredients and methods affect the outcome of each cookie, but I've spelled out how these techniques are used in the recipes throughout this book. My hope is that this will encourage you to experiment and try different methods to achieve your own perfect cookie.

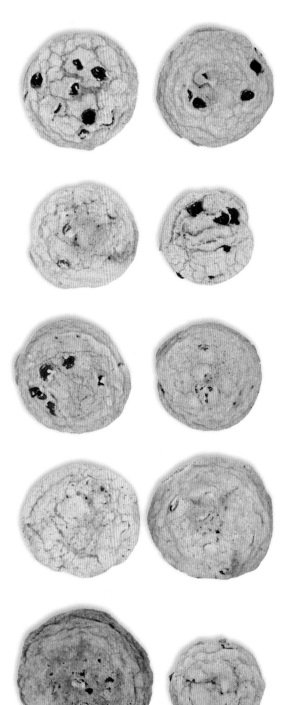

THE GRID

HOW INGREDIENTS AND TECHNIQUE AFFECT COOKIE CREATION

Most chocolate chip cookie recipes start with the same basic ingredients and technique: butter and a mix of granulated and brown sugars are creamed together with vanilla; eggs are beaten in one at a time, followed by flour, salt, and some sort of leavening agent (usually baking soda); the mixture is combined until it just comes together; and then chocolate is added and the dough is scooped onto a baking sheet and baked.

THE SCIENCE BEHIND THE BAKING PROCESS

When you bake a cookie, here's exactly what's going on.

The dough spreads: As the butter warms, it relaxes. The cookie dough begins to melt and gradually spreads out.

The edges set: As the cookie spreads, the edges thin out. This, coupled with the fact that they are fully exposed to the heat of the oven and are constantly reaching hotter areas of the baking sheet, causes the edges to begin to set long before the center of the cookie does.

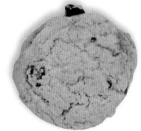

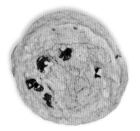 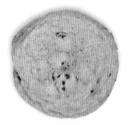

The cookie rises: As the butter melts and the cookie's construction loosens, carbon dioxide gas and water vapor form bubbles that in turn dissolve the baking soda. This baking soda is then able to react with the acidic components of brown sugar, creating gases that cause the cookies to rise and develop a more open interior structure. Salt slows down the decomposition of baking soda, so the bubbles don't get too big.

Egg proteins and starches set: The oven heat causes the butter, egg yolk, and flour to change the shape of the molecules. The gluten in the flour works with the protein and lecithin in the egg, finalizing the shape and size of the finished cookie.

The sugar caramelizes: Heat breaks the sucrose into the simple sugars glucose and fructose, giving each cookie a shiny, light brown crust.

The cookie cools: Once it comes out of the oven, the hot water gases in the cookie contract, which causes the cookie to deflate slightly. The chemical changes that occurred during baking help the cookie keep its shape.

This scientific information is helpful when attempting to change how certain ingredients affect the outcome of your cookies.

"THE CONSTANT" CHOCOLATE CHIP COOKIE RECIPE

●○○○○ MAKES: 14 TO 16 COOKIES

Here is the simple recipe that is the base of our exploratory modifications.

$1/2$ cup salted butter (1 stick), room temperature
$1/2$ cup sugar
$1/2$ cup light brown sugar, firmly packed
1 egg, room temperature
1 teaspoon vanilla extract
1 teaspoon baking soda
$1/2$ teaspoon salt
$1^1/2$ cups all-purpose flour
$3/4$ cup semi-sweet chocolate chips

Preheat oven to 350 degrees F and line a large baking sheet with parchment paper or a silicone baking mat.

In the bowl of an electric mixer fitted with the paddle attachment, cream together butter, sugar, and brown sugar until it turns into a paste-like consistency. Scrape down the bowl.

Mix in the egg and vanilla until smooth. Add baking soda and salt and mix until combined. Add flour and mix until just combined.

Remove the bowl from the electric mixer. Using a rubber spatula, scrape down the bowl and add the chocolate chips.

Use a regular cookie scoop to scoop the dough. Place 10 to 12 dough balls onto the baking sheet, spaced an inch or two apart.

Bake for 9 to 10 minutes until the edges of the cookies are crisp and the centers look puffy and slightly underdone. Remove from the oven and allow to cool on the baking sheet before transferring them to a cooling rack. Continue to bake the rest of the cookie dough.

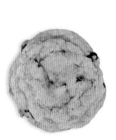 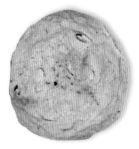

BUTTER

CREAMED BUTTER = LIGHTER AND FIRMER
MELTED BUTTER = DENSER AND CHEWIER
COLD BUTTER = FLAKY LAYERS
EUROPEAN BUTTER = DEPTH OF FLAVOR
BROWN BUTTER = NUTTY FLAVOR

First, butter keeps cookies tender. When flour is mixed with water (such as the water found in eggs), it develops gluten. Gluten can't form in fat, thus butter will inhibit its overall formation, leading to more tender results. The higher the proportion of butter to other ingredients, the more tender your cookies will be (and, consequently, the more they will spread as they bake).

Because of shortening's different melting qualities (and the fact that it has no water content), shortening-based cookies come out softer but denser than those made with butter. The County Fair Chocolate Chip Cookie on page 33 lends a very soft texture but is missing the nutty butterscotch notes that a butter-based cookie brings.

TEMPERATURE

How butter is incorporated can also affect texture. In the early creaming stages of making a cookie, cool butter is beaten until it's light and fluffy. During the process, some air is incorporated, and some of the sugar dissolves in the butter's water phase. This air, in turn, helps leaven the cookies as they bake, giving them some lift (try the Monster Chocolate Chip Cookies on page 60). Melting butter before combining it with sugar and eggs leads to denser cookies like in the Classic Chocolate Chip Cookies on page 28. The temperature of the butter affects how well it holds air. Warm butter flows very easily and doesn't trap bubbles well. The cooler it is, the more viscous it becomes, and the better it can trap air. The recipes in this book will call for different temperatures of butter to create different results.

Most of the recipes in this book call for room temperature butter because it incorporates smoothly into dough, forming a stable foundation for cookies. Room temperature butter is cool to the touch at about 65 degrees F, and when you gently press it, you should be able to make a small indention with your finger. Butter should soften in thirty minutes to an hour by simply leaving it out on the counter. You can also safely leave butter on the counter at room temperature overnight if you know you'll be baking the next day. To bring butter to room temperature quickly, place a stick of butter on a microwave-safe

MELTED BUTTER

MELTED AND COOLED

COLD BUTTER

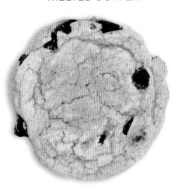

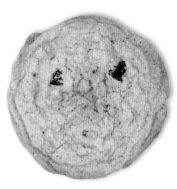

plate and microwave at 20 percent power in ten-second intervals, rotating between each interval until the butter has softened to the touch.

Some recipes call for melted butter. You can effectively melt butter on the stovetop or in the microwave. If melting in the microwave, place the butter in a microwave-safe bowl with a small sheet of parchment paper or paper towel over the top of the bowl to prevent splatter created by air bubbles popping in the butter. When using melted butter in a recipe, allow the butter to cool to room temperature before incorporating it into the dough. This will prevent curdling eggs or melting chocolate chips.

SALTED V. UNSALTED

Most of the recipes here call for unsalted butter—butter without salt added to it. This is a great base for cookie recipes because *you* control the amount of salt added to the recipe. I do like to use salted butter in certain recipes though for an added depth of flavor—those recipes will take that added salt into account with the measurements of the other ingredients.

EUROPEAN BUTTER

European butter has been churned longer to achieve at least 82 percent butterfat and often ferments, giving it a tangy, slightly sour taste. More butterfat makes for a richer flavor but also means a softer texture, faster melt, and often a saturated yellow hue. American-style butter has 80 percent butterfat and no added cultures, creating a more neutral base.

That extra-rich flavor is great in recipes where you want the butter flavor to stand out, like in the Brown Butter White Chocolate Chip Macadamia Nut Cookies on page 52.

BROWN BUTTER

Browning the butter before adding it to the mixture gives the cookies a much more pronounced nuttiness. In order to brown the milk proteins in the butter, you have to evaporate the water content (see page 16 about browning butter). Thus, brown butter adds no moisture to your dough, meaning the sugar in the dough cannot dissolve, which makes it difficult to melt into the cookie. In order to get the sugar to dissolve and caramelize properly, you must add another liquid (like an additional egg) as in the Brown Butter Espresso Dark Chocolate Chip Cookies on page 114.

> **KATIE'S TIP:** When a recipe calls for room temperature butter, I prefer it to sit on the counter overnight, but you can pull it out of the refrigerator 30 minutes before use. Butter can be kept out at a cool room temperature for 24 hours. To bring butter to room temperature quickly, place the stick of butter in a microwave-safe bowl and microwave at 20 percent power in 10-second intervals, rotating between each interval, until the butter has softened to the touch.

EUROPEAN BUTTER

BROWN BUTTER

BUTTER BEAT UNTIL PALE

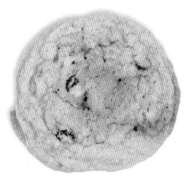

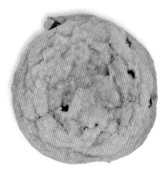

HOW TO MAKE BROWN BUTTER

Brown butter is regular butter that has been cooked just long enough to toast the milk solids found in the butter. By cooking the butter just a tiny bit past the melting point, you create a nutty, caramelized flavor.

1.

To brown butter, melt the butter called for in the recipe in a saucepan over medium heat.

2.

When it boils, reduce heat to low, then simmer until foamy.

3.

Continue cooking, stirring occasionally and scraping the bottom of the pan, until the foam subsides, the butter turns golden brown with a nutty aroma, and the milk solids separate into brown specks that sink to the bottom, about two to seven minutes (depending on amount of butter used).

4.

Remove from heat and immediately transfer to a heatproof bowl, scraping the little brown bits from the bottom of the pan. Let cool to room temperature before using in the recipe.

VANILLA

Most recipes in this book call for pure vanilla extract. There are a handful that call for imitation vanilla. What's the difference? The main difference between pure and imitation vanilla flavoring is how the two extracts are made. Pure or real vanilla extract must contain vanilla beans, water, and alcohol to be called "pure." Imitation extract must also contain these three ingredients but can also have other flavors to boost the vanilla taste. Imitation vanilla holds a stronger vanilla flavor in the final baked cookies than pure vanilla extract, which can mellow during the baking process. In almost all cases, vanilla extract and imitation vanilla are interchangeable.

EGGS

EXTRA EGG WHITES = TALLER COOKIES
EXTRA EGG YOLKS = FUDGIER COOKIES

Egg whites provide a good amount of water, as well as protein. Egg proteins trap and retain bubbles of air or water vapor. The higher the proportion of egg white in a cookie, the more it rises during baking. Because of the extra water, you also get more gluten formation, which again leads to a taller cookie (provided you use enough flour to absorb that extra water). Other than the small amount in the butter, eggs are the main source of water in a cookie dough recipe.

Egg yolks also provide some moisture and protein, but more importantly they provide a well-emulsified source of fat. When cooked, egg yolk forms a tender protein coagulum that can keep cookies tender and fudge-like. A high proportion of egg yolk leads to a more brownie-like texture in a finished cookie. That's why the Brownie Chocolate Chip Cookies recipe on page 103 calls for three eggs.

1 WHOLE EGG

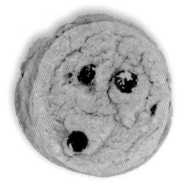

1 EGG + 1 EGG YOLK

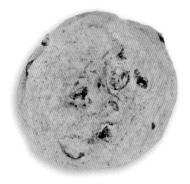

TEMPERATURE

WARMER DOUGH = WIDE COOKIES
COOLER DOUGH = COMPACT COOKIES

Now, let's talk temperature. Cookies baked straight from the fridge will stay a little more compact, while those that are allowed to warm will spread more. By adjusting the starting temperature of the cookie dough and the temperature of the oven, you can create a wide variety of textures and contrasts. Oven temperature matters too: When cookies are baked at a lower temperature, the dough has more of a chance to spread out, leading to flatter, wider cookies. Conversely, cookies baked at higher temperatures spread less. When cookies are baked straight from the refrigerator (or freezer), bake them

at a lower temperature (325 degrees F) to allow them to spread correctly. Cookie dough balls can be stored in the freezer for up to three months.

The longer you can let your dough rest in the refrigerator, the more intense the flavors become. The recipe for The Cookie That Started It All on page 26 is a prime example. Allowing the dough to rest lets flour proteins and starches break down a bit, resulting in a cookie that bakes up darker and more flavorful with outstanding butterscotch notes.

REFRIGERATED DOUGH

FROZEN DOUGH

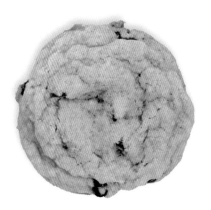

SUGAR

Granulated sugar is crystallized sucrose. It is mildly hygroscopic (likes to retain moisture) and relatively neutral in pH.

Brown sugar (a mixture of white sugar and molasses) is *mostly* crystallized sucrose, but it also contains a good amount of glucose and fructose (making it more likely to absorb moisture from the air than granulated sugar), along with trace minerals that give it its flavor and a slightly acidic pH.

Slightly acidic brown sugar reacts with baking soda, causing cookies to rise higher when baking, which limits their spread. You end up with a cakier result. Granulated sugar, on the other hand, adds no leavening power, so you end up with a cookie that spreads wide. Because granulated sugar–based cookies readily give up moisture, they also end up crispier.

The Thin and Crispy Chocolate Chip Cookies recipe on page 38 calls for $1^1/2$ cups of granulated sugar and only $1/4$ cup of brown sugar, creating that thin, crisp texture. Alternately, the recipe for Nutella-Stuffed Chocolate Chip Cookies on page 104 contains no granulated sugar and only brown sugar, creating a larger, moist cookie.

Recipes in this book call for light or dark brown sugar. The difference is simply the amount of molasses added to the sugar. Dark brown sugar contains nearly twice as much molasses as light, which gives it a richer caramel flavor. Light brown and dark brown sugar can be substituted for each other; the flavor and color of your cookies will change slightly. You can combine white granulated sugar with molasses to make a brown sugar equivalent in a pinch: mix 1 cup of sugar with 1 tablespoon of molasses.

$3/4$ BROWN SUGAR +
$1/4$ SUGAR

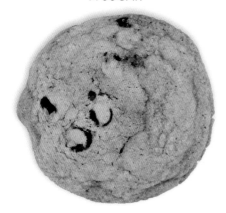

ALL BROWN SUGAR

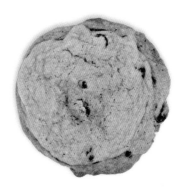

LEAVENING AGENT

BAKING SODA = ROUGH AND COARSE
BAKING POWDER = CAKEY AND SMOOTH

Baking soda is pure sodium bicarbonate. When dissolved in liquid and combined with an acid, it rapidly reacts, breaking down into sodium, water, and carbon dioxide.

Baking powder, on the other hand, is baking soda with powdered acids built right in. When liquid is added, the powdered acid and base dissolve and react with each other, creating bubbles of carbon dioxide without the need for an external acid source. Most baking powders these days are double acting, which means that they contain two different powdered acids. One reacts immediately upon mixing with water, and the other only reacts after it has been heated, giving cakes and cookies a little boost early in the baking phase.

Baking powder generally produces cakier cookies that rise higher during baking, producing smoother, shinier tops, while baking soda yields cookies that are rougher and denser in texture.

In most recipes, the acid in the brown sugar is enough to react with the baking soda and make the cookies rise. Some recipes, however, like the Chocolate Candy Cookies on page 34, call for both baking soda and baking powder. The baking powder does most of the leavening, and the baking soda is added to neutralize the acids in the recipe as well as to add tenderness and some leavening.

When cornstarch is added to a cookie recipe, the starch molecules work to absorb water and thicken the dough. When heated, those molecules swell and consume even more of the liquid in the cookie creating a crunchy exterior. The cornstarch also helps soften the rigid proteins of the flour, resulting in a light and chewy center.

BAKING SODA

BAKING SODA +
BAKING POWDER

+ CORNSTARCH

FLOUR AND METHOD

Since flour provides the bulk of the structure in a cookie, the amount you use can alter the texture of the cookie. A small amount of flour compared to butter (a ratio of 1 to 1 or less) will give you cookies that spread out into a waferlike lace cookie. Extra flour (a ratio of 1.3 to 1 or higher) will give you cookies that barely spread at all as they bake, with centers that stay dense and doughlike, even after being almost fully cooked.

The Oatmeal Chocolate Chip Lace Cookies on page 40 call for only ¾ cup of flour, creating a lacey oatmeal cookie you can practically see through, whereas the Brown Butter Malted Milk Toffee Chocolate Chip Cookies on page 54 require 2 cups of flour for a dense, doughy texture.

HOW TO INCORPORATE

Not only does the amount of flour matter, but *how* you incorporate the flour makes a difference. After adding flour to your batter, if you overwork the dough, you subsequently create a stronger gluten network, and the cookies can end up too tough. Thus, recipes state "mix until just combined, being careful not to overmix" to avoid an unwanted tough texture.

MEASURING

The most accurate way to measure flour is with a kitchen scale (1 cup of flour = 4.2 ounces or 120 grams). If a scale is unavailable, measure the flour's volume precisely: Start by fluffing the flour in the bag or canister. Flour settles easily, becoming tightly packed inside a bag or jar. *Don't* scoop the flour directly from the canister; dipping the measuring cup into the bag or jar will yield too much flour. To make sure you're not scooping up packed flour, fluff it up with a spoon or fork before you measure it. Next, spoon the flour into the measuring cup. Gently pile it in until it forms a heap above the rim of the measuring cup. Don't pack the flour down. Scrape a knife across the top of the measuring cup to level it. This will get rid of excess flour on the top of the cup without packing down the flour inside.

HEAT-TREAT

Consuming raw flour has been linked to salmonella. Thus, when making recipes for edible cookie dough, it's important to heat-treat the flour before using it in a recipe. To do so, preheat the oven to 350 degrees F and line a large baking sheet with parchment paper or a silicone baking mat. Spread the flour in an even layer over the paper. Bake for 5 to 7 minutes. Allow the flour to cool completely, then sift it to break up any clumps that may have formed while baking.

1 CUP OF FLOUR

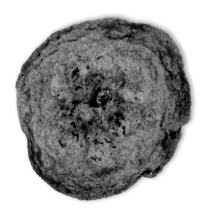

1½ CUPS OF FLOUR

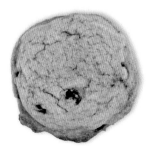

2 CUPS OF FLOUR

HOW TO STORE CHOCOLATE CHIPS:
As a general rule, you want to make sure
your chocolate chips are kept in a cool, dry
location. The ideal temperature is between
60 and 75 degrees F, and they need to be in
an airtight bag or container. Temperature
fluctuation can cause the sugar or fat in
chocolate to bloom, creating white or
gray streaks or spots. Chocolate that has
"bloomed" is still safe to eat.

If stored properly, milk chocolate chips
will stay fresh for approximately one year
after opening the bag. Chips with a higher
concentration of dark chocolate, 60 percent
or higher, will last longer. If they're carefully
stored, semi-sweet, bittersweet, or dark
chocolate chips will last for up to two years.

KATIE'S TIP: My favorite chocolate to use
in cookies is the Guittard Super Cookie Chips.
They are a hybrid between a baking wafer and
a chocolate chip with a 48 percent semi-sweet
to dark chocolate ratio.

CHOCOLATE

Back in the 1930s, innkeeper Ruth Wakefield had a hit on her hands when she chipped a Nestlé's semi-sweet chocolate bar into "pea-size" pieces and baked them into brown sugar cookies at the Toll House Inn in Whitman, Massachusetts, just south of Boston. She is credited with "inventing" the chocolate chip cookie. Nestlé bought the rights to the recipe for Wakefield's chocolate chip Toll House Cookies, printed it on the 7-ounce bar wrapper, and even scored the chocolate bar to help home cooks break it into chips. In 1940, when Nestlé created chocolate morsels (the company's name for chips), Wakefield's recipe went on the back of the bag, where it can still be found today.

Today, we have an abundance of chocolate "chip" options in the baking aisle at the grocery store, so let's break down how chocolate is actually made and determine the best options for chocolate chip cookies.

Chocolate is obtained from cacao beans. The cacao beans are harvested, cleaned, and dried in the sun. They are then roasted and undergo several steps to remove the cacao nibs. These nibs are then ground into a cocoa mass and liquefied. This liquid is known as chocolate liquor, which then gets further processed into cocoa solids and cocoa butter. Cocoa butter is a white cocoa mass that is the base of every type of chocolate. Cocoa solids are what give certain chocolates their dark brown color and bitter flavor. The ratio of cocoa butter to cocoa solids is what determines the type of chocolate.

White Chocolate: White chocolate is the sweetest chocolate available on the market. It consists of cocoa butter, sweetener, and milk but no cocoa solids. This means that there is no brown color imparted in the mixture, which gives the chocolate a silky cream color.

Milk Chocolate: Milk chocolate is also sweet chocolate that consists of cocoa butter, sweetener, milk, or powdered milk, but also between 20 and 35 percent cocoa solids.

Dark Chocolate: Dark chocolate has two classifications: semi-sweet and bittersweet. **Semi-sweet chocolate** is defined as chocolate with a cocoa solid content of between 35 and 65 percent. **Bittersweet chocolate** has a cocoa solid content ranging between 65 and 80 percent, which means it contains more solids and much less sugar than white, milk, or semi-sweet chocolate.

So, what's the best chocolate option for chocolate chip cookies? To make a long story short, it's all about personal preference. Semi-sweet remains the go-to choice for most people. Milk chocolate creates a silky texture but can sometimes be considered too sweet to put into cookies. Dark chocolate contains a bitterness that complements the sweetness of the cookie dough.

Chips vs. chopped: When baking cookies, it's important to consider not only the chocolate type but also the chocolate form/shape. **Chocolate chips** are manufactured to hold their shape through the baking process. They're mainly stabilized using lecithin, creating a slightly waxy texture, allowing the chips to remain as is, even after you pull the cookies out of the oven. **Chopped chocolate** allows the chocolate to melt and meld into the cookie. Rough chopped chocolate results in larger chunks juxtaposed against micro-fragments and tiny shards that envelop the whole cookie, not only changing the appearance of the cookie but the texture as well, making it more dense and fudge-like. **Chocolate disks** are flattened in shape (like candy melts), giving you a relatively even dispersal of chocolate throughout the cookie. Because of their higher cocoa butter content, they tend to melt easier, leading to a flatter cookie with large pools of melted chocolate.

1.

THE CLASSICS

THE COOKIE THAT STARTED IT ALL

●●○○○ MAKES: 12 TO 14 LARGE (5-INCH) COOKIES

It was this very recipe that sparked the idea for this book. When I published my first book *So Much to Celebrate* in 2018, this was the first recipe I included. It was without a doubt the number one recipe people made from the book and the one that they couldn't wait to tell me how much they enjoyed. After a record number of Instagram messages declared undying loyalty to this recipe, I started to think, *What if my second book was just about chocolate chip cookies?* Crazy? Maybe. Brilliant? You tell me.

Even after creating over 100 recipes for this book and baking tens of thousands of chocolate chip cookies, I still return to this recipe as one of my favorites. I love chocolate chip cookies that are soft and chewy in the center, crisp on the edges, sweet with brown sugar, salty with a crunch, and perfectly speckled with just the right amount of chocolate.

So, without further ado, here's the cookie that started it all . . .

1 cup (2 sticks) unsalted butter, melted
1 cup light brown sugar, firmly packed
3/4 cup sugar
2 eggs, room temperature
2 teaspoons vanilla extract
1 teaspoon baking soda
1 teaspoon baking powder
1 teaspoon kosher salt
3 cups all-purpose flour
8 ounces semi-sweet chocolate baking disks
Flaky sea salt, for garnish

Allow time for overnight refrigeration.

1. In the bowl of an electric mixer fitted with a paddle attachment, cream the butter, brown sugar, and sugar together on medium speed until light and fluffy, about 3 to 4 minutes. Add the eggs, one at a time, and mix to combine. Add the vanilla, mix, then scrape down the bowl. Add the baking soda, baking powder, and salt and mix until fully combined. Add the flour all at once and mix it in short bursts until just combined (do not overmix). Add the chocolate pieces and mix on low speed until just mixed in. Cover the bowl with plastic wrap and chill in fridge for a minimum of 24 hours and up to 3 days.

2. Preheat oven to 350 degrees F and line two baking sheets with parchment paper or silicone baking mats. Form the dough into 3 1/2-ounce balls, a little larger than a golf ball. Arrange the balls of dough very far apart on the sheets (cookies will be up to 5 inches wide once baked) and sprinkle the tops of each with a few flecks of sea salt.

3. Bake one cookie sheet at a time for 12 to 17 minutes until golden all over. Remove from the oven and allow to cool on the baking sheet before transferring them to a cooling rack. Continue to bake the rest of the cookie dough.

KATIE'S TIP: This cookie dough can be made up to three days in advance and left to cool in an airtight container in the refrigerator. Cookies are best served the day of baking.

SINGLE CHOCOLATE CHIP COOKIE

●OOOO MAKES: 1 GIANT COOKIE

This is the Carrie Bradshaw of chocolate chip cookies—fun, cool, self-sufficient, perpetually single. When you're all alone and you have a craving for chocolate chip cookies, reach for this recipe. Party of one—sometimes the best kind of party.

2 tablespoons (1/4 stick) salted butter, melted and slightly cooled

3 tablespoons light brown sugar, firmly packed

Pinch of salt

1 egg yolk, room temperature

1/4 teaspoon vanilla extract

1/3 cup all-purpose flour

1/8 teaspoon baking soda

4 tablespoons chocolate chips, divided

1. Preheat oven to 350 degrees F and line a large baking sheet with parchment paper or a silicone baking mat.

2. In a medium bowl, whisk together the butter and brown sugar until combined. Add the salt, egg yolk, and vanilla and whisk until smooth. Switch to a rubber spatula and add the flour and baking soda, stirring until just combined. Fold in 3 tablespoons of the chocolate chips.

3. Shape the dough into a 3 1/2-inch disk on the prepared baking sheet and gently press the remaining 1 tablespoon of chocolate chips randomly over the top and sides of the cookie.

4. Bake in a preheated oven for 12 to 14 minutes, until the cookie is golden. Serve warm or allow to cool for 3 to 5 minutes on a wire rack before transferring to a cooling rack, then store in an airtight container.

KATIE'S TIP: This is a great recipe to bake in a toaster oven or in an air fryer. Make sure you use parchment paper and keep an eye on it because cooking time may differ depending on the appliance. An air fryer, for example, may only take 5 to 7 minutes to bake this cookie.

CLASSIC CHOCOLATE CHIP COOKIES

●●○○○ MAKES: 12 TO 14 COOKIES

When you think of a chocolate chip cookie—this is it. These are soft and chewy on the inside and crisp on the outside. And with a higher salt ratio, these are perfectly salty as well as sweet. This simple, classic recipe will be your family's quintessential go-to chocolate chip cookie recipe.

1¼ cups all-purpose flour

1 teaspoon baking soda

½ teaspoon baking powder

¾ teaspoon salt

½ cup (1 stick) unsalted butter,
  melted and cooled

⅓ cup sugar

½ cup light brown sugar,
  firmly packed

1 egg, room temperature

2 teaspoons vanilla extract

1 cup semi-sweet chocolate chips

1. Preheat oven to 350 degrees F and line a large baking sheet with parchment paper or a silicone baking mat.

2. In a medium bowl, whisk together flour, baking soda, baking powder, and salt. Set aside.

3. In the bowl of an electric mixer fitted with a paddle attachment on medium speed, cream together the cooled butter, sugar, and brown sugar until it turns into a paste-like consistency, about 2 to 3 minutes. Scrape down the bowl.

4. Mix in the egg and vanilla until smooth.

5. Remove the bowl from the electric mixer. Using a rubber spatula, scrape down the bowl and add in the dry ingredients all at once. Stir until just combined, being careful not to overmix.

6. Fold in the chocolate chips.

7. Use a regular cookie scoop to scoop the dough. Place 6 to 7 dough balls onto the baking sheet, spaced 3 inches apart.

8. Bake for 9 to 10 minutes until the edges of the cookies are crisp and the centers look puffy and slightly underdone.

9. Allow them to cool on the baking sheet for 3 to 5 minutes before transferring them to a cooling rack. Continue to bake the rest of the cookie dough.

MINI CHOCOLATE CHIP COOKIES

●●○○○ MAKES: ABOUT 70 COOKIES

I set out to create a recipe for tiny chocolate chip cookies similar to the beloved Chips Ahoy! cookies, and, in my opinion, these are just as snackable. They come out of the oven soft and chewy, but as they cool they become crisp. The imitation vanilla creates that strong vanilla flavor that joyfully lingers in the final cookie.

Be warned: These mini cookies are irresistibly pop-able. You eat two, and before you know it, you've eaten ten. Since the recipe makes 70 cookies, you may be in trouble!

1¹/2 cups all-purpose flour
¹/2 teaspoon salt
1 teaspoon baking soda
¹/2 cup (1 stick) unsalted butter,
　room temperature
¹/3 cup sugar
¹/2 cup light brown sugar,
　firmly packed
1 egg, room temperature
1¹/2 teaspoons imitation
　vanilla extract
3/4 cup mini chocolate chips

1. Preheat oven to 350 degrees F and line a large baking sheet with parchment paper or a silicone baking mat.
2. In a medium bowl, whisk the flour, salt, and baking soda together. Set aside.
3. In the bowl of an electric mixer fitted with a paddle attachment, cream together the butter, sugar, and brown sugar until creamy and smooth.
4. Mix in the egg and vanilla until smooth.
5. Slowly mix in the dry ingredients, until combined. Remove the bowl from the mixer and stir in the mini chocolate chips using a rubber spatula.
6. Use a small cookie scoop to scoop out evenly measured balls of dough. Use a knife to slice those dough balls in half. Using your hands, roll halves into tiny balls, about a teaspoon in size. This method ensures all your cookies will be the exact same size.
7. Place the mini balls on the baking sheet and bake for 6 to 8 minutes or until the cookies are golden brown and set. Remove them from the oven and allow them to cool on the baking sheet before transferring them to a cooling rack. Continue to bake the rest of the cookie dough.

COUNTY FAIR CHOCOLATE CHIP COOKIES

●●○○○ MAKES: 20 TO 24 COOKIES

My in-laws are from rural East Tennessee and have a farmhouse there. This past summer we grew a huge vegetable garden and decided to enter some of our vegetables in the county fair. I saw that there was a chocolate chip cookie competition and just knew I was a dead ringer for a blue ribbon. I made the most over-the-top, giant chocolate chip cookies with European browned butter, Madagascar vanilla, and flaky sea salt on top.

Our eggplants and bell peppers swept their divisions. My cookies didn't even place . . . not even an honorable mention for the city girl trying to compete with the generational country bakers. My problem? I didn't read my audience. I can just envision one of the judges spitting out my highfalutin cookie because he got a crunch of sea salt or tasted brown butter he thought was a sign of a burnt cookie. Know thy audience!

This is the cookie recipe I'll be making for the fair next year, which uses vegetable shortening and imitation vanilla—because the judges at the county fair are looking for a soft cookie with big vanilla flavor like their mamas used to make. Nothing fancy: perfect for the county fair.

3/4 cup all-vegetable shortening

1/4 cup sugar

1 cup light brown sugar, firmly packed

2 tablespoons milk, room temperature

1 egg, room temperature

2 teaspoons imitation vanilla extract

2 cups all-purpose flour

1/2 teaspoon baking soda

3/4 teaspoon salt

1 cup semi-sweet chocolate chips

1. Preheat oven to 350 degrees F and line a large baking sheet with parchment paper or a silicone baking mat.
2. In the bowl of an electric mixer fitted with a paddle attachment, cream together the shortening, sugar, and brown sugar until well blended. Scrape down the bowl and add the milk, egg, and vanilla. Beat until smooth.
3. Add the flour, baking soda, and salt and mix until just combined. Finally, add the chocolate chips and mix one more time very briefly until incorporated.
4. Use a regular cookie scoop to scoop the dough. Place 10 to 12 dough balls onto the baking sheet, spaced 2 to 3 inches apart.
5. Bake for 9 to 10 minutes until the edges of the cookies are crisp and the centers look puffy and slightly underdone.
6. Allow them to cool on the baking sheet before transferring them to a cooling rack. Continue to bake the rest of the cookie dough.

CHOCOLATE CANDY COOKIES

●●○○○ MAKES: 12 TO 14 COOKIES

My kids are obsessed with M&M's. We have a giant glass jar of them in our pantry (right beside the giant jar of chocolate chips). We often put M&M's in my regular chocolate chip cookie recipe per the kids' requests. You can use any kind of chocolate-coated candy, but M&M's are my kids' favorite. I finally decided the candy deserved a recipe of its own and . . . wow. These giant cookies are chewy and buttery and chock-full of chocolatey candy goodness.

$2^1/4$ cups all-purpose flour

1 teaspoon salt

1 teaspoon baking soda

$1/2$ teaspoon baking powder

$3/4$ cup crushed chocolate-coated candies (like M&M's), plus more for garnish

1 cup (2 sticks) unsalted butter, room temperature

$1/2$ cup sugar

1 cup light brown sugar, firmly packed

2 eggs, room temperature

2 teaspoons vanilla extract

Flaky sea salt for garnish

1. Preheat oven to 350 degrees F and line a large baking sheet with parchment paper or a silicone baking mat.
2. In a medium bowl, whisk together the flour, salt, baking soda, and baking powder. Set aside.
3. Fill a zip-top bag with M&M's and seal shut. Cover with a dish towel and use a rolling pin to roughly crush the M&M's into shattered pieces. Set aside.
4. In the bowl of an electric mixer fitted with a whisk attachment, cream together butter, sugar, and brown sugar until it becomes light and fluffy, 2 to 3 minutes. Scrape down the bowl and mix in the eggs one at a time on medium speed. Once combined, scrape down the bowl and mix for another 2 to 3 minutes, then add the vanilla.
5. Scrape down the bowl again and mix in half of the dry ingredients on medium-low speed. Once almost combined, mix in the rest of the dry ingredients on medium-low speed, being careful not to overmix.
6. Pour in the crushed and whole M&M's and use a rubber spatula to gently fold into the dough, being careful not to overmix.
7. Using a large cookie scoop, scoop out the dough and place 6 to 7 dough balls onto the baking sheet, spaced about 3 inches apart.
8. Top with more M&M's and bake for 12 to 15 minutes, until the edges are lightly golden and the centers are pale, puffed, and slightly underdone. While still hot out of the oven, drop the pan onto the counter to deflate the center of the cookies.
9. Sprinkle the cookies with even more whole and crushed M&M's and a pinch of sea salt.
10. Allow to cool on the baking sheet before transferring to a cooling rack. Continue to bake the rest of the cookie dough.

KATIE'S TIP: Crushed M&M's are a must for this recipe. They add great texture and tiny specks of chocolate throughout the cookie.

CAKEY CHOCOLATE CHIP COOKIES

●●○○○ MAKES: ABOUT 34 COOKIES

I am a thin-and-chewy-chocolate-chip-cookie kind of girl. But if you prefer a more cakey cookie, it doesn't mean we can't be friends. I start this recipe by making a traditional cookie base, but at the end I alternate the dry ingredients with buttermilk to make a more cake-like texture. The result is pillowy-soft perfection.

2$\frac{1}{4}$ cups all-purpose flour

1 teaspoon baking soda

1 teaspoon salt

14 tablespoons (1$\frac{3}{4}$ sticks) unsalted butter, room temperature

$\frac{3}{4}$ cup sugar

$\frac{1}{4}$ cup light brown sugar, firmly packed

1 egg, room temperature

2 teaspoons vanilla extract

$\frac{1}{2}$ cup buttermilk

1$\frac{1}{2}$ cups semi-sweet chocolate chips

1. Preheat oven to 350 degrees F and line a large baking sheet with parchment paper or a silicone baking mat.

2. In a small bowl, whisk together the flour, baking soda, and salt. Set aside.

3. In the bowl of an electric mixer fitted with a paddle attachment, combine the butter, sugar, and brown sugar and beat on medium speed until light and fluffy. Reduce speed to low and add the egg and vanilla. Beat until well mixed, about 1 minute. Add half the flour mixture; mix until just combined, then add the buttermilk and mix again until just combined. Add the final half of the flour mixture and mix until just incorporated. Stir in the chocolate chips.

4. Use a medium cookie scoop to scoop the dough. Place 8 to 9 dough balls onto the prepared baking sheet, spaced 2 inches apart.

5. Bake for 10 to 12 minutes, until cookies are golden around the edges and set in the center. Allow them to cool on the baking sheet for 3 to 5 minutes before transferring them to a cooling rack. Continue to bake the rest of the cookie dough.

THIN AND CRISPY CHOCOLATE CHIP COOKIES

●●○○○ MAKES: ABOUT 24 COOKIES

I love big, thick, gooey chocolate chip cookies just like the rest of you, but there is something to be said for a perfectly thin, crisp cookie. This recipe produces a flat, crunchy cookie that just might convert you to a thin-crispy-cookie fan.

2 cups all-purpose flour

1/2 teaspoon baking soda

1 teaspoon salt

1 cup (2 sticks) unsalted butter, room temperature

1 1/2 cups sugar

1/4 cup light brown sugar, firmly packed

2 eggs, room temperature

1 tablespoon vanilla extract

3 tablespoons water

4 ounces semi-sweet chocolate baking wafers, chopped into rough pieces

1. Preheat oven to 350 degrees F and line a large baking sheet with parchment paper or a silicone baking mat.

2. In a medium bowl, whisk together flour, baking soda, and salt. Set aside.

3. In the bowl of an electric mixer fitted with a paddle attachment, cream together on medium speed the butter, sugar, and brown sugar until light and fluffy, 2 to 3 minutes. Scrape down the bowl.

4. Add the eggs, vanilla, and water and mix on low speed to combine. Add the flour mixture all at once and mix on low speed until combined. Add the chocolate and mix on low speed until just incorporated.

5. Use a cookie scoop to scoop the dough. Place 5 or 6 balls about 3 inches apart on the prepared baking sheet.

6. Bake for 9 to 10 minutes until the cookies are golden brown. Allow them to cool on the baking sheet for about 10 minutes before transferring them to a cooling rack. The cookies will crisp as they cool. Continue to bake the rest of the cookie dough.

KATIE'S TIP: These cookies spread quite a bit. Make sure to space your cookie dough balls a good amount apart so they don't meet during baking. You may also need to use a round cookie cutter to round out the edges of the warm dough (see technique on page 7).

OATMEAL CHOCOLATE CHIP LACE COOKIES

●●○○○ MAKES: ABOUT 30 COOKIES

This is one of the first cookie recipes I ever tried baking on my own as a child. It was in my mom's 1977 Nashville Junior League mustard yellow spiral-bound cookbook. This simple recipe creates the most beautifully thin, chewy cookie. I added mini chocolate chips to the recipe, which gives the perfect hint of chocolate speckled through this lacey oatmeal cookie.

$^3/_4$ cup sugar, divided

$^1/_2$ teaspoon cinnamon

$^1/_2$ cup (1 stick) unsalted butter, room temperature

$^1/_2$ cup light brown sugar, firmly packed

1 egg, room temperature

$^1/_2$ teaspoon vanilla extract

$^3/_4$ cup all-purpose flour

$^1/_2$ teaspoon baking soda

$^1/_2$ teaspoon salt

$1^1/_2$ cups quick oats

1 cup mini semi-sweet chocolate chips

KATIE'S TIP: What's the difference between rolled oats and quick oats? Both are steamed and then rolled flat, but quick oats are rolled much thinner than rolled oats. Rolled oats will result in more texture and chewiness inside the baked goods. Quick oats are great for this recipe because the oat pieces are smaller and doughier with less whole-shaped oats inside the crumb. If you have only old-fashioned rolled oats, pulse the oats in a food processor a few times to give them the same texture as quick oats.

These cookies are best when eaten the same day.

1. Preheat oven to 350 degrees F and line a large baking sheet with parchment paper or a silicone baking mat.
2. In a small bowl, combine $^1/_4$ cup of the sugar and cinnamon. Set aside.
3. In the bowl of an electric mixer fitted with a paddle attachment, blend the butter, the remaining $^1/_2$ cup of sugar, and brown sugar on medium speed until pale in color. Add the egg and vanilla and blend on high speed until mixture is white, light, and fluffy.
4. In a medium bowl, whisk together the flour, baking soda, and salt. Turn off the mixer and add the flour mixture to the butter mixture. Turn the mixer on low speed and mix until just combined. Stir in the oats and chocolate chips.
5. Use a medium cookie scoop to scoop the dough. Drop into the cinnamon sugar mixture and toss to coat.
6. Place 5 or 6 dough balls onto the baking sheet, spaced 3 inches apart as they will spread quite a bit. Leave the rest of the dough out at room temperature.
7. Bake for 9 to 10 minutes until the edges of the cookies are just starting to brown but the centers are still white and look underdone. Do not overbake—cookies will settle as they cool.
8. Allow them to cool on the baking sheet before transferring them to a cooling rack. Continue to bake the rest of the cookie dough.

PEANUT BUTTER CHOCOLATE CHIP COOKIES

●●○○○ MAKES: 8 TO 10 LARGE COOKIES

Look no further for the most perfect peanut butter cookie. These are super soft with a perfectly crisp exterior. They are simple to pull together, and refrigerating them overnight not only deepens the flavor profile but also keeps the edges from getting too crispy when they bake.

1 cup all-purpose flour

1/2 teaspoon baking soda

1/2 teaspoon salt

1/2 cup (1 stick) unsalted butter, room temperature

1/4 cup sugar

3/4 cup light brown sugar, firmly packed

1/2 cup creamy peanut butter

1 egg, room temperature

1 teaspoon vanilla extract

1 cup mini semi-sweet chocolate chips (plus more for topping)

Allow time for refrigeration.

1. In a medium bowl, whisk together flour, baking soda, and salt. Set aside.

2. In the bowl of an electric mixer fitted with a paddle attachment, cream together the butter, sugar, brown sugar, and peanut butter until light and fluffy. Scrape down the bowl.

3. Mix in the egg and vanilla until just combined.

4. Slowly mix in the dry ingredients until just combined, being careful not to overmix.

5. Remove the bowl from the mixer and fold in the chocolate chips.

6. Line a small, rimmed baking sheet with waxed or parchment paper to chill the dough.

7. Use a large cookie scoop to scoop the dough, placing the dough balls side by side on the baking sheet. Gently press the extra chocolate chips into the top of each dough ball. Cover with plastic wrap and place in the refrigerator for at least 4 hours or overnight.

8. When ready to bake, preheat oven to 350 degrees F and line a large baking sheet with parchment paper or a silicone baking mat. Place 4 or 5 dough balls onto baking sheet, spaced 3 inches apart. Place the remaining dough back in the refrigerator until ready to bake the next batch. Bake for 12 to 14 minutes until the edges of the cookies are crisp and the centers look puffy and slightly underdone. The cookies will seem pretty doughy, but they will firm up as they cool.

9. Allow them to cool on the baking sheet before transferring them to a cooling rack. Continue to bake the rest of the cookie dough.

KATIE'S TIP: To refrigerate cookie dough, scoop the dough onto a parchment-lined jelly roll pan. Cover tightly with plastic wrap and refrigerate per directions.

PAN-BANGING CHOCOLATE CHIP COOKIES

●●●○○ MAKES: 12 TO 14 COOKIES

Sarah Kieffer is a blogger and the originator of the pan-banging chocolate chip cookie revolution. For the first time in decades, someone created a new technique in the baking world, which goes against all baking instincts: she instructs you to open the oven multiple times during baking to bang the pan of cookie dough against the counter to stop the cookies from rising. Ultimately, this recipe creates cookies with crisp ripples around the edges and soft, chocolate-filled centers. This is my take on her revolutionary original.

2 cups all-purpose flour

1/2 teaspoon baking soda

3/4 teaspoon salt

1 cup (2 sticks) unsalted butter, room temperature

1 1/2 cups sugar

1/4 cup light brown sugar, firmly packed

1 egg, room temperature

1 1/2 teaspoons vanilla extract

2 tablespoons water

6 ounces semi-sweet chocolate baking wafers, chopped into rough pieces

Allow time for freezing.

1. Preheat oven to 350 degrees F and line three large baking sheets with aluminum foil, dull side up.

2. In a medium bowl, whisk together the flour, baking soda, and salt. Set aside.

3. In the bowl of an electric mixer fitted with a paddle attachment, cream together the butter, sugar, and brown sugar on medium speed until light and fluffy, 2 to 3 minutes. Scrape down the bowl.

4. Add the egg, vanilla, and water and mix on low speed to combine. Add the flour mixture all at once and mix until combined. Add the chocolate and mix until just incorporated.

5. Use a large cookie scoop to scoop the dough. Place 4 or 5 balls about 3 inches apart on a prepared baking sheet. Transfer the baking sheet with dough to the freezer for 15 minutes before baking.

6. Place the chilled baking sheet in the oven and bake 10 minutes, until the cookies are puffed slightly in the center. (After you put the first baking sheet in the oven, put the second one in the freezer.)

7. Lay out a kitchen towel on the kitchen counter. At the 10-minute mark, open the oven using an oven mitt, take out the baking sheet, and hold it about 4 inches above the kitchen towel on the counter. Gently let it drop onto the counter so the edges of the cookies set and the centers of the cookies fall down.

8. Return the pan to the oven until the cookies puff up again, about 2 minutes, and repeat, removing them from the oven and dropping them onto the counter. Repeat a few more times to create ridges around the edges of the cookies. Bake 16 to 18 minutes total, until the cookies have spread out and the edges are golden brown but the centers are much lighter and not fully cooked.

9. Transfer the baking sheet to a wire rack; let cool completely before removing the cookies from the pan.

KATIE'S TIP: This is the only recipe in the book that calls for baking on aluminum foil. Aluminum is a natural heat conductor, which creates cookies with darker, crispier edges.

CUT-OUT CHOCOLATE CHIP COOKIES

●●●○○ MAKES: ABOUT 24 3-INCH CUT-OUT COOKIES

Is there anything more fun than a cut-out sugar cookie decorated for a holiday? Who doesn't love red, white, and blue star cookies for the Fourth of July, red hearts for Valentine's Day, or, of course, all the decorated cut-out cookies for Christmas? But why do sugar cookies get to have all the fun? Here's a recipe that gets chocolate chip cookies in on the action. These cookies keep their shape beautifully and, when decorated, are just as adorable as their sugar cookie counterparts.

1 cup (2 sticks) unsalted butter,
   room temperature
1/4 cup sugar
1/2 cup light brown sugar,
   firmly packed
2 egg yolks, room temperature
1 teaspoon vanilla extract
2 1/2 cups all-purpose flour
1 teaspoon salt
1 1/2 cups mini semi-sweet
   chocolate chips

BUTTERCREAM FROSTING
1 cup (2 sticks) unsalted butter,
   room temperature
2 cups confectioners' sugar
1 teaspoon vanilla extract
Sprinkles, to decorate

KATIE'S TIP: A lot of cut-out dough recipes will tell you to chill the dough and then roll it out and bake the cookies. To save time, skip chilling the dough, go ahead and roll out your newly made dough, cut out the cookies, and then pop the entire tray in the freezer for at least 30 minutes before baking. It saves loads of time and your cookies will turn out perfect every time!

Allow time for freezing.

1. Line two large baking sheets with parchment paper or silicone baking mats.
2. In the bowl of an electric mixer fitted with a paddle attachment, cream together on medium speed the butter, sugar, and brown sugar until light and creamy, about 1 minute.
3. Scrape down the bowl and then add the egg yolks and vanilla. Mix until well incorporated.
4. Gradually mix in the flour and salt, then add the mini chocolate chips. Mix until a dough forms.
5. Remove the bowl from the mixer and dump the dough onto a floured surface. The dough may be a bit crumbly, so use your hands to knead the dough until it comes together.
6. Roll the dough out flat until 1/4-inch thick. Then using whatever cookie cutters you like, cut dough into desired shapes, place on prepared baking sheets, and put sheets directly into freezer for 30 minutes.
7. When ready to bake the cookies, preheat oven to 350 degrees F. Bake each sheet one at a time for 10 to 12 minutes or until just set. Don't overbake these cookies—you want them to set up but remain soft. Allow them to cool on the baking sheet for 3 to 5 minutes before transferring them to a cooling rack. Continue to bake the rest of the cookie dough.
8. To make the buttercream frosting, in the bowl of an electric mixer fitted with a whisk attachment, cream together on medium speed the butter, confectioners' sugar, and vanilla until creamy, about 2 to 3 minutes.
9. Spread the buttercream frosting on top of each cooled cookie. Decorate with sprinkles before the frosting hardens.

INSIDE-OUT CHOCOLATE CHIP COOKIES

●●○○○ MAKES: ABOUT 30 COOKIES

I set out to create a *chocolate* chocolate chip cookie, and instead of using just a classic semi-sweet chip, I thought I'd mix it up with white chips this time. When I pulled them out of the oven, my middle daughter, Joey Kate, exclaimed, "Mom, they're inside out!" And voilà, the Inside-Out Chocolate Chip Cookie was born. It satisfies all those chocolaty cravings: a dark chocolate dough speckled with milk and white chocolate chips. They are best eaten warm, so either grab one just out of the oven before it completely cools or pop one in the microwave for 20 seconds before indulging.

$2^1/3$ cups all-purpose flour

$3/4$ cup dark cocoa powder

1 teaspoon baking soda

$1/2$ teaspoon salt

1 cup (2 sticks) unsalted butter, room temperature

1 cup sugar

1 cup light brown sugar, firmly packed

2 eggs, room temperature

$1^1/2$ teaspoons vanilla extract

$1/2$ cup milk chocolate chips

$1^1/2$ cups white chocolate chips, plus more for finishing

1. Preheat oven to 350 degrees F and line a large baking sheet with parchment paper or a silicone baking mat.

2. In a medium bowl, whisk together the flour, cocoa, baking soda, and salt. Set aside.

3. In the bowl of an electric mixer fitted with a paddle attachment, combine the butter, sugar, and brown sugar. Mix until smooth, about 2 minutes. Add the eggs one at a time, mixing well after each addition. Add the vanilla and mix until combined.

4. Gradually add the flour mixture and beat on low speed until just combined. Use a rubber spatula to stir in the chocolate chips.

5. Use a regular cookie scoop to scoop the dough. Place 10 to 12 dough balls onto the baking sheet, spaced 2 to 3 inches apart.

6. Bake for 9 to 10 minutes until the edges of the cookies are crisp and the centers look puffy and slightly underdone. Do not overbake.

7. While the cookies are warm, gently press extra white chocolate chips into the cookies for presentation.

8. Allow them to cool on the baking sheet before transferring them to a cooling rack. Continue to bake the rest of the cookie dough.

CHOCOLATE CHIP–LESS COOKIES

●●○○○ MAKES: 16 TO 18 COOKIES

Confession: Growing up, I did not like chocolate. Nope . . . in fact, I *hated* chocolate. So when my mom would so kindly make us chocolate chip cookies after school, she would make half the batch without the chocolate chips for me. Turns out, I'm not the only one out there who lacks the chocolate gene. When I posted a preview to this recipe on Instagram, I got a surprising number of messages thanking me for creating the perfect cookie just for them. Don't worry, I now *love* chocolate (a prerequisite to being the author of a chocolate chip cookie book), but this cookie is so full of flavor that you'll never miss it.

10 tablespoons (1^1/4 sticks)
  salted butter
1^1/2 cups all-purpose flour
^{1}/2 teaspoon baking soda
^{1}/2 teaspoon salt
^{1}/4 cup sugar
^{3}/4 cup light brown sugar,
  firmly packed
1 large egg plus 1 large egg yolk,
  room temperature
2 teaspoons vanilla bean paste
1 tablespoon water
Flaky sea salt for garnish

1. First brown the butter until it reaches an amber color (see page 16 for directions). Let cool to room temperature.

2. Preheat the oven to 350 degrees F and line a large baking sheet with parchment paper or a silicone baking mat.

3. In a medium bowl, whisk together the flour, baking soda, and salt. Set aside.

4. In the bowl of an electric mixer fitted with a paddle attachment, cream together cooled brown butter, sugar, and brown sugar until incorporated, about 1 minute. Add the egg and yolk, vanilla bean paste, and water. Increase mixer speed to medium-high, and beat until mixture becomes light and ribbony. Reduce mixer speed to low; add dry ingredients and beat just to combine. You may need to remove bowl from mixer and finish incorporating the flour mixture into the dough by using your hands. Do not overmix.

5. Using a regular cookie scoop, place 8 or 9 dough balls on the prepared baking sheet, spacing about 3 inches apart. Sprinkle with sea salt.

6. Bake 9 to 11 minutes until edges are golden brown and firm but centers are still soft. Allow to cool on the baking sheet before transferring them to a cooling rack. Continue to bake the rest of the cookie dough.

BROWN BUTTER WHITE CHOCOLATE CHIP MACADAMIA NUT COOKIES

●●●○○ MAKES: ABOUT 28 COOKIES

When I was pregnant with my first child, Emmaline, I was determined to bring something special for my nurses the day of the birth. As a Southern lady, I just felt it was improper to show up empty-handed (crazy, I know), and I wanted to preemptively thank them for their help.

I somehow decided on white chocolate chip macadamia nut cookies. Emmaline was over a week late, so I ended up making them four or five times—desperately wanting to deliver fresh cookies—before I actually needed to go to the hospital. I'll never forget nurse after nurse popping into my room to rave about the cookies I had left in their break room. Because of these sweet treats, I'd like to think I'll go down in history as their favorite patient ever!

1 cup (2 sticks) salted
   European-style butter
2¼ cups all-purpose flour
1 teaspoon baking soda
½ teaspoon salt
½ cup sugar
1 cup light brown sugar,
   firmly packed
2 eggs, room temperature
2 teaspoons vanilla extract
1 cup white chocolate chips
1 cup dry roasted macadamia
   nuts, coarsely chopped

1. First brown the butter until it reaches an amber color (see page 16 for directions). Let cool to room temperature.
2. Preheat oven to 350 degrees F and line a large baking sheet with parchment paper or a silicone baking mat.
3. In a medium bowl, whisk together flour, baking soda, and salt. Set aside.
4. In the bowl of an electric mixer fitted with a paddle attachment, cream together the butter, sugar, and brown sugar on medium-high speed for 2 to 3 minutes, or until smooth and creamy.
5. Add eggs and vanilla and mix until well combined.
6. Pour in the dry ingredients and mix on medium-low speed until barely combined. Be careful not to overmix.
7. Remove the bowl from the electric mixer. Using a rubber spatula, fold in the white chocolate chips and nuts.
8. Use a regular cookie scoop to scoop the dough. Place 6 to 8 dough balls onto the baking sheet, spaced 3 inches apart. Bake for 9 to 10 minutes until the edges are a light golden brown and the centers are pale and puffed. Use a large, round biscuit cutter to push in the sides of the cookies, making them perfectly round. Work fast because as the cookies cool, the sides will firm up, which makes it much more difficult to round out your cookies.
9. Allow them to cool on the baking sheet before transferring them to a cooling rack. Continue to bake the rest of the cookie dough.

KATIE'S TIP: If the dough seems a bit runny, place the dough in the refrigerator for 30 minutes until it firms up, and then scoop and bake.

BROWN BUTTER MALTED MILK TOFFEE CHOCOLATE CHIP COOKIES

●●●○○ MAKES: ABOUT 24 COOKIES

These cookies really pack a flavor punch. With brown butter, toffee, and malted milk, there is a deepened flavor profile that is simply perfection. If you want to go even further, refrigerate the dough for 24 to 48 hours, deepening the flavors even more. If you do chill the dough, bake at 325 degrees instead of 350.

1 cup (2 sticks) unsalted butter, divided
1 tablespoon water
2 cups all-purpose flour
1/2 cup malted milk
3/4 teaspoon baking soda
1 teaspoon salt
3/4 cup sugar
1/2 cup dark brown sugar, firmly packed
2 teaspoons vanilla extract
2 eggs, room temperature
1 cup semi-sweet chocolate baking disks, roughly chopped
1/2 cup milk chocolate toffee, chopped (or HEATH Bar bits)
Flaky sea salt, for garnish

1. Preheat the oven to 350 degrees F and line a large baking sheet with parchment paper or a silicone baking mat.
2. Cube 1/2 cup (1 stick) of butter and place in a medium heatproof bowl. Set aside.
3. Melt the other 1/2 cup (1 stick) of butter in a medium saucepan over medium-high heat until it reaches an amber color (see page 16 for directions).
4. Pour the brown butter over the cubed butter and stir until everything is melted and smooth. Once melted, whisk in the 1 tablespoon of water and let cool completely.
5. Meanwhile, whisk together the flour, malted milk, baking soda, and salt in a large bowl. Set aside.
6. In a medium bowl using a whisk, mix the cooled brown butter, sugar, brown sugar, and vanilla until incorporated. Add the eggs, and whisk until fully combined, about a minute until smooth and glossy.
7. Add dry ingredients all at once and use a rubber spatula to mix until just combined. Stir in the chopped chocolate and toffee until just combined.
8. Using a regular cookie scoop, place scoops of cookie dough onto the prepared baking sheet, spacing them 2 to 3 inches apart. Bake for 9 to 11 minutes until the edges are a light golden brown and the centers are pale and puffed. While the cookies are still hot, sprinkle lightly with flaky sea salt.
9. Use a round cookie cutter to help shape the sides of the cookies into perfect circles. (See page 7 for directions.)
10. Allow them to cool on the baking sheet before transferring them to a cooling rack. Continue to bake the rest of the cookie dough.

KATIE'S TIP: Place some flecks of chocolate on top of each warm cookie right when they come out of the oven for picture-perfect meltability. Furthermore, if you love toffee, you can add chopped toffee or HEATH Bar bits to almost any recipe in this book for a little added texture and flavor.

BAKE SALE CHOCOLATE CHIP COOKIES

●●●○○ MAKES: 54 REGULAR COOKIES

Raise your hand if your child has ever come to you around 5 P.M. and told you they need a huge amount of dessert to bring to school the next day for a class event or bake sale. I've certainly been there a time or two! Instead of having to quadruple a recipe, I went ahead and did the work for you—ensuring you'll have at least fifty perfect cookies for the school's bake sale tomorrow.

2 cups (1 pound or 4 sticks) salted butter, room temperature

$1^1/_2$ cups sugar

2 cups light brown sugar, firmly packed

3 teaspoons artificial vanilla extract

3 eggs, room temperature

$1^1/_2$ teaspoons baking soda, dissolved in 1 tablespoon water

1 teaspoon salt

$4^1/_2$ cups all-purpose flour

3 cups semi-sweet super chocolate chips

3 cups mini semi-sweet chocolate chips

Flaky sea salt, for garnish

1. Preheat oven to 350 degrees F and line several large baking sheets with parchment paper or silicone baking mats.
2. In a mixer with a paddle attachment, cream the butter, sugar, and brown sugar together until light and fluffy.
3. Add the vanilla and eggs and mix well. Add the baking soda dissolved in water and salt and mix until combined.
4. Gradually add the flour to the creamed mixture. Stir in the chocolate chips, being careful not to overmix.
5. Using a regular cookie scoop, scoop the dough onto the prepared baking sheets, about 2 inches apart.
6. Bake for 10 to 12 minutes, until the edges are slightly golden. Push in the sides with a cookie cutter while warm to shape. While the cookies are still hot, sprinkle lightly with flaky sea salt.
7. Allow them to cool on the baking sheet for 3 to 5 minutes before transferring them to a cooling rack. Continue to bake the rest of the cookie dough.

KATIE'S TIP: While each pan of cookies is baking, leave the extra cookie dough on the counter. You can bake two cookie sheets at once in the same oven by just rotating them halfway through the baking time.

KITCHEN SINK CHOCOLATE CHIP COOKIES

●●●○○ MAKES: 14 TO 16 COOKIES

These "kitchen sink" cookies are inspired by New York's famous Milk Bar, a dessert shop that specializes in innovative and out-of-the-box creations. Founder Christina Tosi wows customers with her whimsical and nostalgic ingredients. Her Kitchen Sink Cookies include coffee grounds (not espresso powder but fresh coffee grounds), potato chips (I like to use Original Cape Cod for a good crunch), and butterscotch chips. I created a recipe that is a little friendlier for the at-home baker but still remarkably delicious. The sweet/salty combo is mind-blowing.

$2^1/2$ cups all-purpose flour

1 teaspoon baking soda

1 teaspoon baking powder

$1^1/2$ teaspoons salt

1 teaspoon coffee grounds

1 cup (2 sticks) unsalted butter, melted

1 cup light brown sugar, firmly packed

$2/3$ cup sugar

1 tablespoon light corn syrup

1 teaspoon vanilla extract

2 eggs, room temperature

1 cup semi-sweet chocolate chips

$1/2$ cup butterscotch chips

$1/2$ cup graham crackers (about 3 crackers), crushed

$1/3$ cup old-fashioned oats

2 cups potato chips

1 cup mini pretzels, broken into pieces

Flaky sea salt, for garnish

1. Preheat oven to 350 degrees F and line a large baking sheet with parchment paper or a silicone baking mat.
2. In a medium bowl, whisk together the flour, baking soda, baking powder, salt, and coffee grounds. Set aside.
3. In a large bowl of an electric mixer fitted with a paddle attachment, cream together the melted butter, brown sugar, sugar, and corn syrup on medium-high speed until the mixture lightens and thickens, about 3 minutes. Mix in the vanilla and eggs until smooth.
4. Dump in the dry ingredients all at once and mix until just combined.
5. Using a rubber spatula, fold in the chocolate chips, butterscotch chips, graham cracker pieces, oats, potato chips, and pretzel pieces.
6. Using a large cookie scoop, place 7 or 8 dough balls on the prepared baking sheet, spacing about 3 inches apart. Sprinkle with sea salt.
7. Bake for 12 to 14 minutes until the edges of the cookies are crisp and the centers look puffy and slightly underdone. Remove from the oven and allow to cool on the baking sheet before transferring them to a cooling rack. Continue to bake the rest of the cookie dough.

KATIE'S TIP: "Kitchen sink" recipes allow you to put in "everything but the kitchen sink," or anything that you have on hand. Feel free to make this recipe your own. The base is perfect for you to edit the mix-ins.

MONSTER CHOCOLATE CHIP COOKIES

●●○○○ MAKES: 10 TO 12 LARGE COOKIES

These *giant*, soft oatmeal cookies loaded with chocolate and other treats are called monster cookies because they are the Frankenstein monster of the cookie world—a mash-up of oatmeal, peanut butter, and chocolate chip cookies. Just a hint of molasses adds to the chewy texture and deepens the flavor. I add sugar googly eyes after baking just for fun. It's hard not to eat more than one, but who's looking?

1 cup all-purpose flour
1 cup quick oats
1 teaspoon baking soda
1/2 teaspoon salt
1/2 cup (1 stick) unsalted butter,
  room temperature
1/4 cup sugar
3/4 cup light brown sugar,
  firmly packed
1/2 cup creamy peanut butter
1 egg, room temperature
1 teaspoon vanilla extract
2 teaspoons molasses
2 cups monster trail mix
  (a mix of peanuts, M&M's,
  raisins, milk chocolate chips,
  and peanut butter chips)

1. Preheat oven to 350 degrees F and line a large baking sheet with parchment paper or a silicone baking mat.
2. In a medium bowl, whisk together the flour, oats, baking soda, and salt. Set aside.
3. In the bowl of an electric mixer fitted with a paddle attachment, cream together the butter, sugar, brown sugar, and peanut butter until light and fluffy. Scrape down the bowl.
4. Mix in the egg, vanilla, and molasses until just combined.
5. Scrape down the bowl and slowly mix in the dry ingredients until just combined, being careful not to overmix.
6. Remove from the mixer and fold in the monster trail mix.
7. Use a large cookie scoop to scoop the dough. Place 5 or 6 dough balls onto the baking sheet, spaced 3 inches apart.
8. Bake for 12 to 14 minutes until the edges of the cookies are lightly golden.
9. Allow them to cool on the baking sheet before transferring them to a cooling rack. Continue to bake the rest of the cookie dough.

KATIE'S TIP: I like using a monster trail mix because it has everything already included. If you can't find it, you can just use 3/4 cup of a candy like M&M's, 1 cup milk chocolate chips, 1/4 cup peanuts, 1/4 cup raisins, and 1/4 cup peanut butter chips.

SALTED CARAMEL CHOCOLATE CHIP COOKIES

●●●○○ MAKES: 20 TO 24 COOKIES

Salted caramel is a trend that I don't want to end. I just can't get enough! When I imagined this cookie, I really wanted chewy caramel in every bite. I prefer Kraft's baking caramels, and the Kraft Caramel Bits are especially good if you can find them. These cookies are soft on the inside, crisp on the outside, bursting with sweet caramel and creamy chocolate, and contain a little punch of flaky sea salt.

3/4 cup soft baking caramels
   (like Kraft's), chopped
2 1/2 cups all-purpose flour
1/2 teaspoon baking soda
1 teaspoon salt
1 cup (2 sticks) unsalted butter,
   melted and cooled
1/2 cup sugar
1 cup light brown sugar,
   firmly packed
2 eggs, room temperature
1 tablespoon vanilla extract
1 cup dark chocolate chips
1 cup semi-sweet chocolate chips
Flaky sea salt, for garnish

Allow time for refrigeration.

1. If using baking caramels, unwrap each caramel and cut with a sharp knife into quarters to make smaller pieces. Set aside.
2. In a medium bowl, whisk together flour, baking soda, and salt. Set aside.
3. In the bowl of an electric mixer fitted with a paddle attachment, mix together the cooled butter, sugar, and brown sugar until smooth and silky, about 3 minutes.
4. Mix in the eggs and vanilla until smooth.
5. Remove the bowl from the electric mixer. Using a rubber spatula, scrape down the bowl and add in the dry ingredients. Stir until just combined, being careful not to overmix.
6. Fold in the chocolate chips and caramel pieces.
7. Use a regular cookie scoop to scoop dough side by side onto a small baking sheet lined with parchment paper. Refrigerate for at least 4 hours, but preferably overnight.
8. When ready, preheat oven to 350 degrees F and line a large baking sheet with parchment paper or a silicone baking mat. Place 8 or 9 dough balls onto the baking sheet, spaced 2 inches apart.
9. Bake for 10 to 12 minutes, until the edges of the cookies are crisp and the centers look puffy and slightly underdone. Remove from the oven and sprinkle each cookie with flaky sea salt while still hot.
10. Allow them to cool on the baking sheet before transferring them to a cooling rack. Continue to bake the rest of the cookie dough.

FANCY-PANTS BAKERY-STYLE CHOCOLATE CHIP COOKIES

●●●●○ MAKES: 10 TO 12 LARGE COOKIES

If you search "chocolate chip cookie" on Instagram, you'll likely be inundated with images of giant gooey cookies from bakeries all over the world. One of my favorites is the Levain Bakery in New York City. They have become incredibly famous and are an Instagram-worthy photo-op for tourists and locals alike. This recipe is my nod to those extra-large bakery-style cookies with gooey centers, crispy edges, and that rich flavor you just can't put your finger on.

2¼ cups all-purpose flour
1 teaspoon cornstarch
½ teaspoon baking powder
¼ teaspoon baking soda
½ teaspoon salt
1 cup (2 sticks) unsalted European-style butter, room temperature
¼ cup sugar
¾ cup dark brown sugar, firmly packed
1 large egg plus 1 egg yolk, room temperature
1½ teaspoons vanilla bean paste (or 2 teaspoons vanilla extract)
1 cup dark chocolate bar, chopped
¾ cup milk chocolate bar, chopped
Flaky sea salt, for garnish

Allow time for overnight refrigeration.

1. In a medium bowl, whisk together the flour, cornstarch, baking powder, baking soda, and salt. Set aside.
2. In the bowl of an electric mixer fitted with a whisk attachment, cream together the butter, sugar, and brown sugar until it is light and fluffy (about 5 minutes).
3. Scrape down the bowl and add in the eggs and vanilla bean paste. Beat on medium-high speed for about 3 minutes or until pale and creamy.
4. Scrape down the bowl and dump in the dry ingredients and mix on medium-low speed until it's almost combined.
5. Remove the bowl from the stand and add the chocolate. Use a rubber spatula to fold it in and work in the remaining bits of dry ingredients. Do not overmix.
6. Line a small tray with waxed paper to refrigerate the dough. Using a large cookie scoop, place the dough balls side by side on the tray. Let the dough chill overnight, uncovered.
7. To bake, preheat the oven to 350 degrees F and line a large baking sheet with parchment paper or a silicone baking mat. Place 5 cookies on the baking sheet and make sure they're well-spaced apart. Add a couple of extra chocolate chips on top if desired.
8. Bake for 13 to 16 minutes or until the edges are a pale golden color and the centers look dull on the surface but doughy in the middle.
9. Remove from the oven and sprinkle the warm cookies with a pinch of sea salt. Allow to cool on the baking sheet before transferring them to a cooling rack. Continue to bake the rest of the cookie dough.

KATIE'S TIP: This recipe calls for vanilla bean paste, which is a mixture of vanilla powder and vanilla extract ground into a paste, giving it a more syrup-like consistency with vanilla bean specks. It has a more intense vanilla flavor and is available at most grocery stores.

FREEZER CHOCOLATE CHIP COOKIE DOUGH

●●○○○ MAKES: 12 TO 14 COOKIES

Do yourself a favor and store some chocolate chip cookie dough in your freezer. You'll never regret it. When your family gets the craving for homemade cookies, you'll be one step ahead of them. New neighbor? You can stand at their doorstep with warm cookies the afternoon they move in. Your sister's boyfriend just broke up with her and she's on your couch? You're 12 minutes from fixing all her troubles. Trust me . . . freezer chocolate chip cookie dough always comes in clutch.

2¹/4 cups all-purpose flour
1 teaspoon baking soda
¹/2 teaspoon baking powder
¹/2 teaspoon salt
1 cup (2 sticks) salted butter, room temperature
³/4 cup sugar
³/4 cup light brown sugar, firmly packed
2 eggs, room temperature
2 teaspoons vanilla extract
2 cups semi-sweet chocolate chips

Allow time for freezing.

1. In a medium bowl, use a whisk to mix the flour, baking soda, baking powder, and salt. Set aside.
2. In the bowl of an electric mixer fitted with a paddle attachment, cream together on medium speed the butter, sugar, and brown sugar until combined.
3. Beat in the eggs and vanilla until fluffy.
4. Mix in the dry ingredients all at once until just combined. Add in the chocolate chips and mix until just combined.
5. Use a regular cookie scoop to scoop the dough. Place the dough balls side by side on a rimmed baking sheet lined with parchment paper.
6. Cover the baking sheet with plastic wrap and freeze for at least an hour until the dough is hard. Then dump the frozen dough balls into a zip-top bag. Return the sealed bag to the freezer for storage until ready to bake (dough balls can be stored in the freezer for up to 3 months).
7. When ready to bake, preheat oven to 325 degrees F and line a large baking sheet with parchment paper or a silicone baking mat.
8. Place 6 to 7 frozen dough balls onto the baking sheet, spaced 3 inches apart.
9. Bake for 10 to 12 minutes until the edges of the cookies are crisp and the centers look puffy and slightly underdone.
10. Allow them to cool on the baking sheet for 3 to 5 minutes before transferring them to a cooling rack. Continue to bake the rest of the cookie dough.

KATIE'S TIP: When baking dough straight from the freezer or refrigerator, bake at a slightly lower temperature of 325 degrees F, allowing the cookies time to spread.

EDIBLE CHOCOLATE CHIP COOKIE DOUGH

●●○○○ MAKES: ABOUT 2 CUPS OF COOKIE DOUGH

Your best friend just broke up with her boyfriend, and you're putting together a "broken heart" care package. Is there anything better to include than a jar of edible cookie dough? This dough is not meant to be baked—just eaten straight from the fridge. Applesauce serves as a replacement for eggs (trust me, you'll never be able to taste it in the dough), and I like to keep the baking soda in there, not for a rising agent, but for flavor—it really helps add that subtle signature cookie taste.

1³/4 cups all-purpose flour,
  heat-treated (*see page 21)
¹/2 teaspoon baking soda
¹/2 teaspoon salt
11 tablespoons salted butter,
  room temperature
³/4 cup sugar
¹/4 cup light brown sugar,
  firmly packed
¹/4 cup applesauce
1 teaspoon vanilla extract
1 cup semi-sweet chocolate chips

Allow time for refrigeration.

1. In a medium bowl, whisk together the flour, baking soda, and salt. Set aside.
2. In the bowl of an electric mixer fitted with a paddle attachment, cream together the butter, sugar, and brown sugar until incorporated, about 1 minute. Add the applesauce and vanilla; increase the mixer speed to medium-high and beat until the mixture becomes light. Reduce the mixer speed to low; add the dry ingredients and beat just to combine. Add the chocolate chips and mix until just combined.
3. You can use a cookie scoop to form balls or place the dough in an airtight container. Refrigerate for at least 30 minutes before serving and store in the fridge.

ONE-MINUTE CHOCOLATE CHIP COOKIE

●○○○○ MAKES: 1 SERVING

Sometimes you *need* a freshly baked chocolate chip cookie, but you're just not feeling the messy kitchen, hot oven, 30-minute prep time, 12-minute bake time, or sink full of dirty dishes that comes with it. You're in luck. This recipe makes one cookie serving right in a mug and only requires one minute in the microwave. Yes, you read that right . . . you're one minute away from a warm chocolate chip cookie. You're welcome.

1 tablespoon unsalted butter, melted
1 tablespoon sugar
1 tablespoon dark brown sugar, firmly packed
1 egg yolk
1/8 teaspoon vanilla extract
Pinch of salt
1/4 cup all-purpose flour
2 tablespoons milk chocolate chips

1. Very lightly coat the inside of a 6-ounce mug or ramekin with a tiny bit of cooking spray or butter. In the prepared mug, use a spoon to mix the butter, sugar, and brown sugar. Add the egg yolk and vanilla and mix until smooth. Add the salt and flour and mix until just incorporated. Fold in the chocolate chips.

2. Using a 1,000-Watt microwave, microwave for 1 minute at 80 percent power. The top will look light and yellow and may even seem undercooked, but if you gently press the top and it lightly springs back, it's perfect.

3. Serve immediately while it's warm with a scoop of vanilla ice cream.

2.

SPECIALTY COOKIES AND BARS

CHOCOLATE CHIP COOKIE CANDY BARS

●●○○○ MAKES: ABOUT 18 BARS

A chocolate chip cookie crust layered with sweet caramel and topped with chocolate and crunchy pretzels makes for the most impressive homemade candy bars—similar to a Snickers. Don't be fooled, though—this recipe is incredibly simple and fun to make. They're easy to package in cellophane bags, making them a great gift for friends and family.

$1/2$ cup (1 stick) unsalted butter, room temperature

1 cup sugar

1 egg

1 teaspoon vanilla extract

$1^{1}/2$ cups flour

$1/2$ teaspoon baking soda

$1/2$ teaspoon salt

1 cup semi-sweet mini chocolate chips

2 (10 ounce) bags caramels, unwrapped

$1/4$ cup heavy cream

$3/4$ cup roasted peanuts, roughly chopped

12 ounces milk chocolate, chopped

1 tablespoon coconut oil

20 to 24 pretzel twists

Allow time for refrigeration.

1. Preheat the oven to 350 degrees F and line a 9 x 13-inch baking pan with parchment paper.
2. In a large mixing bowl, using a rubber spatula, beat together the butter and sugar until combined. Add the egg, beating until combined and creamy. Beat in the vanilla. Add the flour, baking soda, and salt and beat until combined. Stir in the chocolate chips.
3. Spread the dough out into a thin layer in the prepared pan and bake for 18 to 20 minutes, until just set in the center. Let cool.
4. Meanwhile, melt the caramels and heavy cream in a heatproof bowl in the microwave in 30-second increments, stirring in between until smooth. Stir the peanuts into the caramel. Gently pour the caramel over the cooled cookie crust. Let set 10 to 15 minutes.
5. Melt the chocolate and coconut oil together in the microwave in a heatproof bowl in 30-second increments, stirring in between until smooth. Pour the chocolate mix over the peanut-caramel layer. Press the pretzels into the chocolate.
6. Transfer the bars to the fridge and chill 1 hour, until set (or 30 minutes in the freezer). Cut into bars and store at room temperature in an airtight container.

WHITE CHOCOLATE CHIP BLONDIES

●○○○○ MAKES: ABOUT 16 BARS

I have been making these blondies for over twenty years, and they are certainly a crowd favorite. They're buttery, chewy, speckled with pecans, and they totally stand up on their own without being compared to their brownie counterpart.

$3/4$ cup white chocolate chips
$1/2$ cup (1 stick) unsalted butter
$3/4$ cup sugar
2 eggs, room temperature
$1^1/2$ teaspoons pure vanilla extract
$1/8$ teaspoon salt
$1^1/2$ cups all-purpose flour
1 cup pecans, chopped

1. Preheat the oven to 325 degrees F and line a 9 x 9-inch pan with parchment paper.
2. In a heatproof bowl, microwave the white chocolate chips and butter on high for 30-second increments, stirring between each until melted and smooth (it's okay if the chocolate and butter mixture seems separated). Allow to cool 1 to 2 minutes.
3. Add the sugar and, using a rubber spatula, stir until well incorporated. Stir in the eggs and vanilla until combined. Add the salt, flour, and pecans and stir until well incorporated and the nuts are evenly dispersed.
4. Pour batter into the prepared baking pan and bake for 35 to 40 minutes, or until golden brown and the center is still soft. Let cool completely before slicing into 2-inch squares. Best served at room temperature.

KATIE'S TIP: These are great when made the day before and stored in an airtight container at room temperature.

RICE CRISPY TREAT CHOCOLATE CHIP COOKIES

●●○○○ MAKES: 24 COOKIES

Rice Krispies Treats are a childhood staple for a reason: they're delicious, indulgent, and so easy to make. It doesn't feel right that just a few ingredients could make something so good. This takes the perfect salty-sweet, gooey-crunchy deliciousness of a Rice Krispies Treat and puts it right into the heart of a chocolate chip cookie.

1 cup (2 sticks) unsalted butter, room temperature
1/2 cup sugar
1 cup dark brown sugar, firmly packed
2 eggs, room temperature
2 teaspoons vanilla extract
2 1/4 cups all-purpose flour
1 teaspoon baking soda
1/2 teaspoon baking powder
1 teaspoon salt
2 cups crispy rice cereal
1 cup mini semi-sweet chocolate chips
About 9 regular-sized marshmallows, cut in half
Pinch of sea salt

1. Preheat oven to 350 degrees F and line a baking sheet with parchment paper or a silicone baking mat.
2. In the bowl of an electric mixer fitted with a paddle attachment, beat the butter with the sugar and brown sugar for several minutes until pale and creamy, scraping down the bowl as needed.
3. Add the eggs one at a time, followed by the vanilla, mixing and scraping the bowl after each egg is added.
4. Add the flour, baking soda, baking powder, and salt and mix until the dough just starts to come together.
5. Add the crispy rice cereal and the chocolate chips and mix until just combined.
6. Use a large cookie scoop to scoop the dough. Place 4 to 5 dough balls onto the baking sheet, spaced 3 inches apart.
7. Place a half of a marshmallow into the center of each cookie dough portion. Use your hands to work the dough around the marshmallow so that the marshmallow is completely concealed inside. Sprinkle with extra crispy rice cereal pieces and a pinch of sea salt.
8. Bake for 8 to 10 minutes, just until the cookies start to turn golden brown but before the marshmallows melt completely. The marshmallows will puff out of the tops of the cookies as they bake, and if you bake them too long, they will melt and disappear completely.
9. Allow the cookies to cool on the baking sheet for 3 to 5 minutes before transferring them to a cooling rack. Continue to bake the rest of the cookie dough.

KENTUCKY DERBY PIE CHOCOLATE CHIP COOKIE BARS

●●●○○ MAKES: ABOUT 16 BARS

Southerners take the Kentucky Derby very seriously—almost as seriously as they take pie. These bars are a cookie/pie hybrid that celebrates the best of both worlds: a doughy cookie crust topped with a sticky, sweet filling made with bourbon and chocolate chips, then covered by a crunchy pecan top.

CHOCOLATE CHIP
COOKIE LAYER

3/4 cup (1 1/2 sticks) salted butter,
    room temperature
1/2 cup light brown sugar,
    firmly packed
1/2 cup sugar
2 eggs, room temperature
1 1/2 teaspoons vanilla extract
2 cups all-purpose flour
3/4 teaspoon baking soda
1/2 teaspoon salt
1 cup semi-sweet chocolate chips

PECAN PIE LAYER

3 eggs, room temperature
1 cup light corn syrup
1/4 cup dark brown sugar,
    firmly packed
1 tablespoon bourbon
1 cup semi-sweet chocolate chips
2 cups roasted pecans
Flaky sea salt, for garnish

1. Preheat oven to 350 degrees F and grease a 9 x 13-inch baking pan or line with parchment paper.

2. To make the cookie layer, in the bowl of an electric mixer fitted with a paddle attachment, beat together the butter, brown sugar, and sugar until combined. Add the eggs, one at a time, beating until combined and creamy. Beat in the vanilla. Add the flour, baking soda, and salt and beat until just combined. Stir in the chocolate chips. Spread the dough out in the prepared dish in an even layer.

3. To make the pecan pie layer, in a medium bowl, whisk together the eggs, corn syrup, brown sugar, and bourbon until smooth. Stir in the chocolate chips and pecans.

4. Carefully pour the pecan mixture over the cookie layer. It's okay if not everything is covered. Use a spoon to move pecans around to evenly distribute.

5. Bake for 35 to 40 minutes, until the top is golden brown. It's okay if the center is a little jiggly; it will firm up as it cools. Top with a pinch of flaky sea salt while still warm.

6. Transfer the pan to a wire rack and let cool completely (about an hour). Use the parchment paper to gently lift from the pan. Cut into bars and serve.

BANANAS FOSTER CHOCOLATE CHIP COOKIES

●●●○○ MAKES: 12 TO 14 COOKIES

I can remember when I was a little girl and my dad ordered us Bananas Foster at Sperry's Steakhouse in Nashville for the very first time. The waiters did a tableside preparation, igniting the rum the bananas were cooking in into an aroma-rich flame—quite a show for a little girl. To make it even better and more memorable, the dessert tasted spectacular. I really wanted a banana chocolate chip cookie recipe in this book but couldn't land the right one. After several lackluster results, I thought, *What if I caramelize the bananas like in Bananas Foster?* Ta-da! The result are these cookies, which are spectacular—even without the flaming show.

1 cup (2 sticks) unsalted butter

2 large ripe bananas, peeled and roughly chopped

$3/4$ teaspoon ground cinnamon

$2^3/4$ cups all-purpose flour

$1/2$ teaspoon baking soda

$1/2$ teaspoon baking powder

$1/2$ teaspoon salt

$1/4$ cup vegetable shortening

$1^1/4$ cups sugar, divided

$3/4$ cup light brown sugar, firmly packed

2 eggs, room temperature

2 teaspoons vanilla extract

6 ounces semi-sweet chocolate baking disks, roughly chopped

$3/4$ cup pecan halves, roughly chopped

Flaky sea salt, for garnish

KATIE'S TIP: Don't skip rolling the dough in sugar. It adds a delightful crispy texture to the outside of the final cookie.

Allow time for refrigeration.

1. Melt the butter in a medium saucepan over medium heat. Add the bananas and cook, stirring frequently until they begin to fall apart, darken in color to a light golden brown, and are very fragrant, 8 to 10 minutes total. Remove the pan from the heat, stir in the cinnamon, and let cool for 30 minutes.

2. Line 2 large baking sheets with parchment paper or silicone baking mats.

3. In a medium bowl, whisk together the flour, baking soda, baking powder, and salt. Set aside.

4. In the bowl of an electric mixer fitted with a paddle attachment, cream together on medium speed the cooled (but still melted) banana mixture, vegetable shortening, $3/4$ cup of the sugar, and brown sugar until fully combined. Scrape down the bowl and add in the eggs and vanilla. Mix on medium speed until light and ribbony, 2 to 3 minutes.

5. With the mixer on low, gradually add the dry ingredients, and then the chocolate and pecans, mixing until just incorporated.

6. Pour the remaining $1/2$ cup of sugar into a wide bowl. Use a regular cookie scoop to scoop the dough. Roll each dough ball in the sugar and place them 3 inches apart on the prepared baking sheets. Chill the baking sheets in the refrigerator, uncovered, for 30 minutes.

7. While the dough is chilling, preheat oven to 325 degrees F.

8. Bake each sheet for 12 to 14 minutes, until the edges of the cookies are crisp and the centers look puffy and slightly underdone. Remove from the oven and sprinkle the warm cookies with a pinch of sea salt.

9. Allow them to cool on the baking sheet for 3 to 5 minutes before transferring them to a cooling rack. Continue to bake the rest of the cookie dough.

HOT HONEY CHOCOLATE CHIP COOKIES WITH HOT HONEY CARAMELIZED PECANS

●●●○○ MAKES: ABOUT 32 COOKIES

I grew up in Nashville, a city where tourists stand in line for hours for the now-famous hot chicken. Rounding out the recipes for this book, I realized I didn't have a *spicy* cookie. Hot honey is so on trend right now, and I thought the sweet/spicy flavor would work well in chocolate chip cookies. Boy, was I right! These cookies are the perfect balance of sweet and spicy. The chewy, sweet texture is incredible, and the heat builds as it lingers in your mouth.

HOT HONEY CARAMELIZED PECANS
1/4 cup hot honey
1 1/2 teaspoons salt
1/4 cup light brown sugar, firmly packed
1 teaspoon cinnamon
1 teaspoon cumin
3/4 teaspoon cayenne pepper
16 ounces pecan halves

CHOCOLATE CHIP COOKIES
2 1/4 cups all-purpose flour
1 teaspoon baking soda
1/2 teaspoon salt
1 cup (2 sticks) unsalted butter, room temperature
1/2 cup sugar
1/2 cup light brown sugar, firmly packed
1/4 cup hot honey, plus more for drizzling
2 eggs
2 teaspoons vanilla extract
2 cups semi-sweet chocolate disks, chopped
3/4 cup hot honey caramelized pecans, chopped (recipe above)
Cayenne pepper, for garnish
Flaky sea salt, for garnish

1. Start by making the caramelized pecans. Preheat oven to 350 degrees F and line a large baking sheet with parchment paper or a silicone baking mat.
2. Pour the hot honey into a medium bowl and stir vigorously to thin. Whisk in the salt, brown sugar, cinnamon, cumin, and cayenne pepper. Pour in pecans and toss to coat.
3. Bake pecans in a single layer on the baking sheet for 10 minutes.
4. Upon removing from the oven, use a spatula to toss the pecans in the melted honey mixture.
5. Allow to cool completely, then break apart into singles and clusters. Set aside.
6. For the chocolate chip cookies, in a small mixing bowl, mix together the flour, baking soda, and salt.
7. In a large mixing bowl, whisk together the butter, sugar, brown sugar, hot honey, eggs, and vanilla until smooth and creamy.
8. Switch to a rubber spatula and add the flour mixture. Stir until just combined. Stir in the chocolate and pecans.
9. Use a regular cookie scoop to scoop the dough. Place 6 to 8 dough balls on the baking sheet, spaced 3 inches apart.
10. Bake for 9 to 10 minutes until the edges of the cookies are crisp and the centers look puffy and slightly underdone. Fresh out of the oven, sprinkle with just a dusting of cayenne pepper and sea salt.
11. Allow them to cool on the baking sheet for 3 to 5 minutes before transferring them to a cooling rack. Continue to bake the rest of the cookie dough.
12. Once completely cool and just before serving, drizzle each cookie with a small amount of hot honey.

MALTED OATMEAL PECAN CHOCOLATE CHIP COOKIE BARS

●●○○○ MAKES: ABOUT 16 BARS

I literally had an argument with my mom about the ingredient list for these bars. Upon tasting them, she couldn't believe there wasn't coffee included in the batter. The malted milk is the secret ingredient here, and when combined with the oats, pecans, and a large dose of vanilla, it produces an extraordinary flavor that you can't quite put your finger on . . . and can't quite stop eating.

1¼ cups all-purpose flour
¾ cup malted milk powder
¾ teaspoon baking soda
½ teaspoon salt
½ teaspoon cinnamon
1½ cups (3 sticks) unsalted
    butter, melted and cooled
⅓ cup sugar
¾ cup light brown sugar,
    firmly packed
2 eggs, room temperature
1 tablespoon vanilla extract
2 cups rolled oats
1 cup semi-sweet chocolate chips
1 cup chopped pecans
Flaky sea salt

1. Preheat oven to 325 degrees F and grease a 9 x 9-inch baking pan or line with parchment paper.
2. In a medium bowl, whisk together the flour, malted milk powder, baking soda, salt, and cinnamon. Set aside.
3. In a large bowl, whisk together the melted butter, sugar, brown sugar, eggs, and vanilla until the sugar is mostly dissolved.
4. Add the dry ingredients all at once to the butter mixture and stir using a rubber spatula until a smooth dough forms. Mix in the oats, chocolate chips, and chopped pecans until just combined.
5. Pour the batter into the prepared baking pan and spread in an even layer using an offset spatula. Sprinkle with flaky sea salt.
6. Bake for 35 to 40 minutes, covering with foil if you need to keep the cookies from getting too brown on top. To check for doneness, insert a toothpick into the center. The toothpick should come out with crumbs; the batter on the toothpick should not be wet.
7. Transfer the pan to a wire rack and let cool completely. Use the parchment paper to gently lift from the pan. Cut into bars and serve.

KATIE'S TIP: To cut *perfectly* square cookie bars, measure with a ruler to get the exact number of bars you want. Using a sturdy paring knife, lightly score the ends of the bars to correlate with your desired measurements. Prepare your chef's knife for cutting by coating with cooking spray and then wiping clean with a paper towel. Line up the knife with the score marks, starting from the middle of the complete block of bars. Extend the knife across the surface to the other side. Firmly press the knife down through the bars and gently drag to the end closest to you. Repeat this step as many times as needed. With each pass, wipe the knife clean, coat with cooking spray, and wipe clean again.

PEANUT BUTTER CHOCOLATE CHIP COOKIE BARS

●○○○○ MAKES: ABOUT 16 BARS

There's no better match than chocolate chip cookies and peanut butter. These bars are sweet, doughy, and swirled with creamy peanut butter. They are the quintessential after-school treat and a super simple recipe to keep in your baking arsenal.

1 cup (2 sticks) salted butter, room temperature

1/2 cup sugar

2/3 cup light brown sugar, firmly packed

2 eggs

2 teaspoons vanilla extract

2 1/4 cups all-purpose flour

1 teaspoon baking soda

1/2 teaspoon salt

2 cups semi-sweet chocolate chips

3/4 cup creamy peanut butter

Flaky sea salt, for garnish

1. Preheat oven to 350 degrees F and grease a 9 x 9-inch baking pan or line with parchment paper.

2. In a large mixing bowl, whisk together the butter, sugar, and brown sugar until smooth. Add the eggs, one at a time, beating until combined and creamy. Beat in the vanilla. Switch to a rubber spatula and add the flour, baking soda, and salt and beat until combined. Stir in the chocolate chips.

3. Spread the dough out in the prepared dish. Dollop and then gently swirl the peanut butter (I like to use a wooden skewer) into the dough. Sprinkle a few more chocolate chips on top. Transfer to the oven and bake for 20 to 22 minutes, until just set in the center. Sprinkle with flaky sea salt. Let cool and then cut into bars.

KATIE'S TIP: This is a fun one to make with kids. One bowl, simple measurements, and one baking pan make it easy to have the little ones' help. Swirling in the peanut butter is my kids' favorite part.

LEMON AND WHITE CHOCOLATE CHIP COOKIES

●●○○○ MAKES: 16 TO 18 COOKIES

Documenting the creation of this book on Instagram has been a unique experience. My incredible followers at @katiejacobsnashville have cheered me on, laughed with me, and supported me through the sometimes difficult moments of writing a book. Because these great people have been such a huge part of this cookbook, I thought it would be fun to offer an original recipe contest so one of them could actually *be a part* of the book.

Katie Cranfield's recipe and story stood out. She's a doctor from Newcastle-upon-Tyne in the United Kingdom, and she literally wrote me from the hospital while getting ready to birth her second child. Social media has many pitfalls, but it's not lost on me that it brought together two Katies from across the globe—both baking cookies with our little kids up on our counters. Katie created this recipe for her mother and now makes them with her daughter Emily (my daughter's name is Emmaline).

This recipe is elegant and well-balanced, yet bursting with flavor. I hope that one day Katie from the UK and this Katie from the US can share a batch together over a cup of tea.

1¹/₂ cups all-purpose flour

1 teaspoon baking soda

1 teaspoon baking powder

¹/₂ teaspoon salt

¹/₂ cup (1 stick) unsalted butter, room temperature

¹/₂ cup sugar

¹/₂ cup light brown sugar, firmly packed

1 egg, room temperature

1 tablespoon fresh lemon zest (from about 2 lemons)

1 teaspoon lemon extract

³/₄ cup white chocolate chips

³/₄ cup white chocolate bar, chopped (about 1 bar)

1. Preheat oven to 325 degrees F and line a large baking sheet with parchment paper or a silicone baking mat.

2. In a medium bowl, whisk together the flour, baking soda, baking powder, and salt. Set aside.

3. In the bowl of an electric mixer fitted with a paddle attachment, cream together on medium speed the butter, sugar, and brown sugar until it is light and fluffy, about 2 to 3 minutes. Scrape down the bowl.

4. Mix in the egg, lemon zest, and lemon extract until smooth and well combined.

5. Remove the bowl from the electric mixer. Using a rubber spatula, scrape down the bowl and add in the dry ingredients all at once. Stir until just combined, being careful not to overmix.

6. Fold in the white chocolate chips and chopped white chocolate.

7. Use a regular cookie scoop to scoop the dough. Place 6 to 8 dough balls on the baking sheet, spaced 3 inches apart.

8. Bake for 9 to 12 minutes until the edges of the cookies are crisp and the centers look puffy and slightly underdone.

9. Allow them to cool on the baking sheet for 3 to 5 minutes before transferring them to a cooling rack. Continue to bake the rest of the cookie dough.

KATIE'S TIP: To ensure lemon flavor in your final cookies, use lemon extract (found at the grocery next to the vanilla) instead of fresh lemon juice as the juice will bake out and the oils in the extract will keep the flavor.

WHITE CHOCOLATE CHIP GINGER MOLASSES COOKIES

●●○○○ MAKES: 24 TO 28 COOKIES

Growing up in Nashville, we always went to Becker's Bakery on 12th Avenue for old-fashioned birthday cakes made with shortening and beautifully piped flowers. They had giant glass cases of cookies in the front of the bakery, and my brother and I always got to pick out a cookie while my mom paid for the cake. My brother loved their chewy molasses cookies that had a candied cherry in the center of each. This recipe is a dead ringer for those super chewy, dense molasses cookies—minus the cherry but with added white chocolate.

2²/3 cups all-purpose flour

1 teaspoon baking soda

¹/2 teaspoon salt

1¹/2 teaspoons ground cinnamon

1 teaspoon ground ginger

¹/2 teaspoon ground nutmeg

¹/8 teaspoon ground cloves

1 cup (2 sticks) unsalted butter, room temperature

³/4 cup dark brown sugar, firmly packed

¹/2 cup sugar

1 egg, room temperature

¹/3 cup unsulphured molasses

1 teaspoon vanilla extract

1 cup white chocolate chips, roughly chopped

COATING

¹/2 cup turbinado sugar

1 teaspoon ground cinnamon

1. Preheat oven to 350 degrees F and line a large baking sheet with parchment paper or a silicone baking mat.

2. In a medium bowl, whisk together the flour, baking soda, salt, and spices. Set aside.

3. In the bowl of an electric mixer fitted with a whisk attachment, cream together the butter, brown sugar, and sugar on medium-high speed for 2 to 3 minutes or until smooth, light, and fluffy.

4. Scrape down the bowl and add the egg, molasses, and vanilla and mix again on the same speed for another 2 to 3 minutes. The mixture should be silky, light, and creamy.

5. Pour in half of the dry ingredients and mix on medium-low speed until barely combined. Scrape down the bowl and then pour in the rest of the dry ingredients. Mix again on that same medium-low speed until just combined.

6. Remove the bowl from the electric mixer. Using a rubber spatula, fold in the chopped white chocolate chips.

7. In a separate small bowl, combine the sugar and cinnamon to make the coating.

8. Use a regular cookie scoop to scoop the dough and toss each ball in the cinnamon-sugar mixture for coating.

9. Place 5 or 6 dough balls onto the baking sheet, spaced 3 inches apart. Bake for 9 to 10 minutes until the edges are a light golden brown and the tops are cracked and crinkly. The cookies will darken, flatten, and settle as they cool.

10. Allow them to cool on the baking sheet before transferring to a cooling rack. Continue to bake the rest of the cookie dough.

KATIE'S TIP: Unsulphured molasses is made from ripe sugar cane and doesn't require any sulphur dioxide to preserve it. In general, unsulphured molasses is the more commercial "purest," cleaner-tasting molasses.

PEPPERMINT WHITE CHOCOLATE CHIP CHOCOLATE COOKIES

●●○○○ MAKES: ABOUT 24 COOKIES

I always make all my neighbors (new and old) tins of cookies around the holidays with our family Christmas card attached to the outside of the tins. It's a wonderful way to say "Merry Christmas," visit our old neighborhoods, and keep in touch with the incredibly kind families we've gotten to know over the years. These peppermint-speckled cookies are a must, along with the White Chocolate Chip Ginger Molasses Cookies on the previous page.

Go ahead and bookmark this recipe—you'll want to add it to your holiday baking. One bite and—*BAM!*—it's Christmas.

1 cup semi-sweet chocolate chips

2 tablespoons water

1/2 cup (1 stick) unsalted butter

1/2 teaspoon vanilla extract

1/2 teaspoon peppermint extract

2 eggs, room temperature

3/4 cup sugar

1/2 cup light brown sugar, firmly packed

1 cup all-purpose flour

2 tablespoons natural, unsweetened cocoa powder

1 teaspoon baking powder

1/2 teaspoon salt

1 cup white chocolate chips

1/2 cup crushed peppermint, about 3 candy canes

KATIE'S TIP: When we were growing up, my mom would have us all sit around the kitchen counter, unwrapping candy canes, one by one, and adding them to a plastic zip-top bag to be crushed by a rolling pin. Nowadays, you can buy crushed peppermint at the grocery store around the holiday season or year-round online.

1. Preheat oven to 350 degrees F and line a large baking sheet with parchment paper or a silicone baking mat.

2. In a medium heatproof bowl, microwave the chocolate chips, water, and butter in 30-second increments, stirring in between, until chocolate and butter are completely melted and smooth. Add in the vanilla and peppermint extracts, stir until smooth, and set aside to cool completely.

3. In the bowl of an electric mixer fitted with a whisk attachment, add the eggs, sugar, and brown sugar. Whip on high speed until the egg mixture is pale yellow and ribbony and has almost tripled in volume, about 5 minutes.

4. While the egg mixture is whipping, in a medium bowl, whisk together the flour, cocoa powder, baking powder, and salt.

5. Reduce the mixer speed to low and slowly pour the melted chocolate mixture into the egg mixture. Mix until just combined, then turn the mixer off and add the flour mixture. Stir with a rubber spatula until just combined. The dough will be very soft. Fold in the white chocolate chips.

6. Use a medium cookie scoop to scoop the dough. Place 5 or 6 dough balls onto the baking sheet, spaced 3 inches apart. Sprinkle the tops of the dough balls with crushed peppermint candy canes.

7. Bake for 9 to 10 minutes until the tops of the cookies are cracked and shiny but still slightly underdone. Remove from the oven and sprinkle each cookie with more finely crushed peppermint candy canes.

8. Allow cookies to cool on the baking sheet before transferring to a cooling rack. Continue to bake the rest of the cookie dough.

BROWN BUTTER BOURBON PECAN CHOCOLATE CHIP COOKIES

●●○○○ MAKES: 24 TO 26 COOKIES

An Old Fashioned is my drink of choice—warm spicy bourbon mixed with a little sugary sweetness. If my favorite cocktail married a chocolate chip cookie, this would be their love child. This is a soft, chewy cookie with bourbon and brown butter undertones, speckled with chocolate and crunchy, sugared pecans. Drinks (and cookies) are on me.

1 cup raw pecan halves

2 tablespoons bourbon, divided

1 tablespoon, plus $^3/_4$ cup light brown sugar, firmly packed

1 cup (2 sticks) salted butter, room temperature, divided

$^1/_4$ cup sugar

2 eggs, room temperature

1 teaspoon vanilla extract

$2^1/_4$ cups all-purpose flour

1 teaspoon baking soda

$^1/_2$ teaspoon salt

$1^1/_2$ cups semi-sweet chocolate chips

Flaky sea salt, for garnish

1. Preheat oven to 350 degrees F and line a baking sheet with parchment paper. On the baking sheet, combine the pecans, 1 tablespoon of the bourbon, and 1 tablespoon of the brown sugar. Bake 8 to 10 minutes, until toasted. Let cool completely and roughly chop. Set aside.

2. While the pecans are roasting, brown the butter until it reaches an amber color (see page 16 for directions). Let cool to room temperature.

3. In the bowl of an electric mixer fitted with a paddle attachment, beat together the butter, $^3/_4$ cup of the brown sugar, and the sugar until combined. Beat in the eggs, one at a time, until combined. Add the remaining 1 tablespoon of bourbon and the vanilla, and beat until creamy. Add the flour, baking soda, and salt. Fold in the chocolate chips and chopped pecans mixture (holding back a few of each to place on the tops of the cookie dough balls). The dough will be a little sticky.

4. Use a medium cookie scoop to scoop the dough. Place 8 to 10 dough balls onto the baking sheet, spaced about 2 inches apart. Top the dough balls with the remaining chocolate and chopped pecans mixture.

5. Bake for 9 to 10 minutes until the edges of the cookies are crisp and the centers look puffy and slightly underdone. Remove from the oven and sprinkle each cookie with flaked sea salt while still hot.

6. Allow them to cool on the baking sheet for 3 to 5 minutes before transferring them to a cooling rack. Continue to bake the rest of the cookie dough.

KATIE'S TIP: The bourbon brown sugar–glazed pecans are key here—don't skip that step. They add that smoky bourbon flavor that makes the cookies so unique.

BROWN BUTTER TRIPLE CHOCOLATE CHIP COOKIES

●●●○○ MAKES: 10 LARGE COOKIES

In the process of creating this book, I have tested and tried almost every chocolate available at the grocery store. I love Tony's Chocolonely fair-trade Belgian chocolate bars. They are huge, thick bars of chocolate wrapped in brightly colored paper, usually available in the specialty chocolate section (but also available online). I love using three different flavored chopped-up chocolate bars in this cookie recipe—the high-quality chocolate melts beautifully into the cookie, creating a different flavor profile with every gooey bite. Don't worry if you can't find Tony's—any high-quality chocolate bars will work here—just use a mix of dark, semi-sweet, and milk chocolate.

1 cup (2 sticks) unsalted butter, room temperature

2 cups all-purpose flour

1 teaspoon baking soda

1/2 teaspoon salt

1/3 cup sugar

1 cup light brown sugar, firmly packed

2 eggs, room temperature

2 teaspoons vanilla extract

1/2 cup dark chocolate bar, chopped

1/2 cup milk chocolate hazelnut bar, chopped

1/2 cup dark milk chocolate bar, chopped

Flaky sea salt for garnish

1. Preheat the oven to 350 degrees F and line a large baking sheet with parchment paper or a silicone baking mat.

2. First brown the butter until it reaches an amber color (see page 16 for directions). Let cool to room temperature.

3. In a medium bowl, whisk together the flour, baking soda, and salt. Set aside.

4. In the bowl of an electric mixer fitted with a whisk attachment, cream together the cooled brown butter, sugar, and brown sugar until incorporated, about 1 minute. Add the eggs and vanilla. Increase the mixer speed to medium-high, and beat until mixture lightens and begins to thicken, about 3 minutes. Reduce the mixer speed to low. Add the dry ingredients and beat just to combine. Mix in the chocolate pieces with a rubber spatula. Let the dough sit at room temperature at least 30 minutes to allow the flour to hydrate.

5. Using a large cookie scoop, place 5 dough balls on the prepared baking sheet, spacing about 3 inches apart. Sprinkle with sea salt.

6. Bake 9 to 11 minutes until the edges are golden brown and firm but the centers are still soft. Allow to cool on the baking sheet before transferring them to a cooling rack. Continue to bake the rest of the cookie dough.

KATIE'S TIP: Use a serrated knife to chop the chocolate bars. The serrations on the blade of a serrated knife are much better at grabbing the smooth surface of a chocolate bar than a chef's knife or paring knife.

BROWN BUTTER MAPLE PUMPKIN CHOCOLATE CHIP COOKIES

●●●○○ MAKES: 10 LARGE COOKIES

When fall finally rolls in, I am one of those people who craves all things pumpkin. These chocolate chip cookies are giant pillows—incredibly soft and tender with hints of pumpkin spice. Don't skip the sugar coating, which adds a little crunch and sweetness, or the chocolate baking wafers, which create puddles of chocolate throughout the soft cookie.

1 cup (2 sticks) salted butter, browned and cooled

1 tablespoon water

2 1/4 cups all-purpose flour

1 teaspoon baking soda

1/2 teaspoon baking powder

1/2 teaspoon salt

1 teaspoon pumpkin pie spice

1/2 teaspoon cinnamon

1 cup dark brown sugar, firmly packed

1 egg yolk, room temperature

3 tablespoons maple syrup

1 teaspoon vanilla extract

1/3 cup pumpkin puree

1/2 cup semi-sweet chocolate baking disks, chopped

COATING

2 tablespoons light brown sugar, firmly packed

2 tablespoons sugar

1 teaspoon cinnamon

1. Preheat oven to 350 degrees F and line a large baking sheet with parchment paper or a silicone baking mat.
2. Brown the butter until it reaches an amber color (see page 16 for directions). Whisk the water into the warm butter and let cool to room temperature.
3. In a medium bowl, whisk together the flour, baking soda, baking powder, salt, pumpkin pie spice, and cinnamon. Set aside.
4. In a separate bowl, whisk together the brown sugar and cooled brown butter.
5. Whisk in the egg yolk, maple syrup, vanilla, and pumpkin puree until smooth.
6. Add the dry ingredients to the pumpkin mixture and fold batter with a rubber spatula until combined. Stir in the chocolate until just combined.
7. In a small bowl, combine the coating ingredients.
8. Use a large cookie scoop to scoop the dough. Drop into the cinnamon-sugar mixture and toss to coat. The dough will be very soft.
9. Place 5 dough balls onto the baking sheet, spaced 3 inches apart. Leave the rest of the dough out at room temperature.
10. Bake for 12 to 14 minutes until the edges of the cookies are crisp and the centers look puffy and slightly underdone.
11. Allow them to cool on the baking sheet before transferring them to a cooling rack. Continue to bake the rest of the cookie dough.

KATIE'S TIP: Make sure you use canned 100 percent pumpkin puree for this recipe. Do not use canned pumpkin pie filling, as it contains sugar and extra spices.

MINT CHOCOLATE CHIP COOKIES

●●●○○ MAKES: ABOUT 16 LARGE COOKIES

My favorite ice cream in the whole world is mint chocolate chip. So why wouldn't I make a mint chocolate chip cookie? No, I'm not talking about a food-colored green cookie with no taste . . . but an elevated cookie bursting with real mint flavor. I get my mint straight from my garden (if you've ever grown mint, you know you can't get rid of it, so why not use it?). These soft giant cookies are infused with mint and speckled with both white chocolate and semi-sweet chocolate, giving them a cool, smooth burst of flavor.

1 cup (2 sticks) unsalted butter

1/2 cup packed fresh mint leaves

1/2 cup sugar

1 1/3 cups light brown sugar, firmly packed

2 eggs, room temperature

1 teaspoon vanilla extract

1/2 teaspoon peppermint extract

3 cups all-purpose flour

1 teaspoon baking powder

1 teaspoon baking soda

3/4 teaspoon salt

6 ounces white chocolate bar, roughly chopped

6 ounces semi-sweet chocolate disks, roughly chopped

1. First brown the butter until it reaches an amber color (see page 16 for directions). Remove from the heat, add the mint leaves, and let cool at room temperature for 30 minutes, stirring occasionally.

2. Preheat oven to 350 degrees F and line 2 large baking sheets with parchment paper or silicone baking mats.

3. Strain the butter over the mint through a fine-mesh sieve into the bowl of an electric mixer. Press down on the mint with a spoon to squeeze out all the butter, then discard the mint. With the mixer fitted with a whisk attachment, add the sugar and brown sugar and whisk on medium to combine. Add the eggs, vanilla, and peppermint extract and whisk on medium until ribbony (once you lift the whisk, thick ribbons will fall from it) and smooth, about 1 minute.

4. Remove the bowl from the mixer and add the flour, baking powder, baking soda, and salt, and stir with a rubber spatula just until dough forms. Mix in both chopped chocolates.

5. Use a large cookie scoop to scoop the dough. Place about 6 dough balls onto the prepared baking sheet, spaced about 3 inches apart.

6. Bake each sheet for 13 to 16 minutes until the edges of the cookies are crisp and the centers look puffy and slightly underdone. Immediately bang the cookie sheet on the countertop as soon as they come out of the oven to deflate the cookies slightly.

7. Allow them to cool on the baking sheet for 3 to 5 minutes before transferring them to a cooling rack. Continue to bake the rest of the cookie dough.

KATIE'S TIP: Let this recipe be a jumping off point for your imagination. You can infuse butter with many different aromatics before baking. Vanilla, cardamom, and rosemary would add a great depth of flavor to any cookie or cake.

BROWNIE CHOCOLATE CHIP COOKIES

●●●○○ MAKES: 24 TO 28 COOKIES

Chocolate chip cookies and brownies are best friends. They share similar ingredients and baking methods, but the final results are uniquely different. So what if we took the best parts of a brownie and put them into a chocolate chip cookie? The result? Gooey, fudgy, brownie-cookie perfection.

2 cups all-purpose flour
1/4 teaspoon baking powder
3 eggs, room temperature
1 1/4 cups sugar
3/4 teaspoon salt
1 teaspoon vanilla extract
5 tablespoons unsalted butter
1 cup semi-sweet chocolate chips
2 tablespoons coconut oil
1/4 cup cocoa powder
1 cup milk chocolate chips

1. Preheat oven to 350 degrees F and line a large baking sheet with parchment paper or a silicone baking mat.
2. In a small bowl, whisk together the flour and baking powder and set aside.
3. In the bowl of a stand mixer fitted with a paddle attachment, beat the eggs, sugar, and salt on medium-high speed until the mixture is pale and frothy, about 2 to 3 minutes. Turn the mixer to low speed and stir in the vanilla until just combined.
4. While the egg mixture is beating, melt the butter by placing it in a small microwave-safe bowl and heating until just melted. Add the semi-sweet chocolate and coconut oil and continue to heat until melted, pausing to stir frequently, until smooth. Remove from the microwave and add in the cocoa powder; whisk until completely combined.
5. Add the warm chocolate-butter mixture to the egg mixture and mix on low speed until combined. Add the flour mixture and mix on low speed until combined. Let the mixture set at room temperature for 5 minutes. Stir in milk chocolate chips until just combined.
6. Use a regular cookie scoop to scoop the dough. Place 6 to 8 dough balls onto the prepared baking sheet, spaced 3 inches apart.
7. Bake for 9 to 10 minutes until the edges of the cookies are crisp and the centers look puffy and slightly underdone.
8. Allow them to cool on the baking sheet for 3 to 5 minutes before transferring them to a cooling rack. Continue to bake the rest of the cookie dough.

NUTELLA-STUFFED CHOCOLATE CHIP COOKIES

●●●○○ MAKES: 10 TO 12 LARGE COOKIES

At my house, we are a little obsessed with hazelnut spread (Nutella is our favorite), so I was determined to somehow work it into chocolate chip cookies. The tricky part? Nutella is so gooey and sticky—how would I create a cookie where it holds up through the baking process? The answer—the freezer! Freezing balls of Nutella before surrounding them with cookie dough creates just what I was looking for—a cookie with an ooey-gooey, hazelnutty center!

Roughly $1/3$ cup hazelnut spread
   (like Nutella)
2 cups all-purpose flour
1 teaspoon baking soda
$1/2$ teaspoon salt
$3/4$ cup unsalted butter,
   room temperature
$1^1/4$ cups light brown sugar,
   firmly packed
1 egg plus 1 egg yolk,
   room temperature
2 teaspoons vanilla extract
4 ounces dark chocolate,
   finely chopped

Allow time for freezing.

1. Start by prepping the Nutella. Line a plate with waxed paper and use a small cookie scoop to scoop out 12 heaping teaspoons onto the plate. Pop these balls in the freezer to firm up while you start on the dough.
2. Preheat the oven to 375 degrees F and line a large baking sheet with parchment paper or a silicone baking mat.
3. For the dough, in a large bowl, whisk together the flour, baking soda, and salt. Set aside.
4. In the bowl of an electric mixer fitted with a paddle attachment, mix together the butter and brown sugar until light in color.
5. Next, mix in the egg, egg yolk, and vanilla.
6. Mix in the dry ingredients until just incorporated. Remove the bowl from the mixer and use a rubber spatula to fold in the chopped chocolate.
7. Using a large cookie scoop, fill it about halfway with the cookie dough then press your thumb in the center to create a well. By this time, the Nutella balls you placed in the freezer should be solid enough to pick up. Press a frozen Nutella ball into the center, then cover with more cookie dough. Make sure you create a tight seal, so the Nutella doesn't melt out. Place 2 inches apart on the prepared baking sheet.
8. Bake for 10 to 12 minutes or until the edges are golden brown. The center will still look a little doughy.
9. Allow them to cool on the baking sheet before transferring them to a cooling rack. Continue to bake the rest of the cookie dough.

KATIE'S TIP: This recipe would also work great with peanut butter instead of Nutella. Freeze balls of peanut butter and then wrap in cookie dough to create a gooey peanut butter center.

CHOCOLATE CHIP COOKIE SHORTBREAD

●●●○○ MAKES: ABOUT 30 COOKIES

I am a huge shortbread fan, and I must tell you that I struggled with this recipe. On my fourth or fifth attempt, I was complaining on Instagram that I might have to scratch the idea altogether. I didn't want to just add chocolate chips to a shortbread recipe. Rather, I was really hoping to create a shortbread cookie that was inspired by chocolate chip cookies. That's when one of my followers, Linda Fuson, came to the rescue with a recipe she had gotten from a friend years ago and had kept on a handwritten recipe card. The verse "Taste and see that the Lord is good. Psalm 34:8" was printed on the bottom. The Lord *is* good, and so is this recipe! With just a few tweaks, I baked three batches of shortbread and did a little happy dance in my kitchen at the outcome.

18 tablespoons (2¼ sticks) salted butter, room temperature
½ cup sugar
¼ cup light brown sugar, firmly packed
1 teaspoon vanilla extract
2¼ cups all-purpose flour
¾ cup semi-sweet mini chocolate chips
1 egg, for coating the dough
Coarse sugar (turbinado) for coating dough
Flaky sea salt, for garnish

Allow time for refrigeration.

1. In the bowl of an electric mixer fitted with a paddle attachment, cream together the butter, sugar, brown sugar, and vanilla until light and fluffy, 3 to 5 minutes. Scrape down the bowl.
2. With the mixer on low speed, slowly add the flour. After the flour is all incorporated, add in the chocolate chips and mix until just combined.
3. Divide dough into two large balls. Make the balls into two logs about 12 inches long. Place on plastic wrap and completely wrap each log. Slice open an empty cardboard paper towel roll, and place each plastic-wrapped dough log one at a time inside to perfectly form the round log—about 2 inches thick. Refrigerate the dough for 2 hours.
4. When ready to bake, preheat oven to 350 degrees F and line a large baking sheet with parchment paper or a silicone baking mat.
5. Remove the dough logs from the refrigerator. One at a time, unwrap each log and use a knife to slice it in half short-wise, to create 4 logs total. In a small bowl, beat the egg and then brush it over the sides of the log. Immediately roll the egg-washed log in the turbinado sugar (this gives the cookies a crispy, sugary edge). Then slice each log into ½- to ¾-inch rounds with a serrated knife and place each cookie on the prepared cookie sheet only about an inch apart. Lightly sprinkle each cookie with a pinch of sea salt.
6. Bake for 9 to 10 minutes until the edges of the cookies begin to darken. Do not overbake. You *do not* want the edges to brown, only to begin to darken. Remove from the oven and allow to cool on the baking sheet before transferring them to a cooling rack. Continue to bake the rest of the cookie dough.

CHOCOLATE CHIP COOKIE BROWNIES

●●●○○ MAKES: ABOUT 16 BROWNIES

This is a two-for-one recipe! It's brownie batter layered on top of chocolate chip cookie dough—quite possibly the two best things in the world combined! The best part? This story has a choose-your-own ending. You can stop at the chocolate chip cookie base layer and bake it for simple Chocolate Chip Cookie Bars that have a caramel undertone from the combination of melted butter and dark brown sugar. Or take it a step further and top the cookie dough layer with brownie batter for ooey-gooey Chocolate Chip Cookie Brownies. Both endings are bliss!

COOKIE DOUGH

1 cup (2 sticks) unsalted butter, melted
$1/2$ cup sugar
1 cup dark brown sugar, firmly packed
1 egg, room temperature
2 teaspoons imitation vanilla
1 teaspoon baking soda
1 teaspoon salt
$2^1/4$ cups all-purpose flour
$1^1/2$ cups semi-sweet chocolate chips

BROWNIE BATTER

3 eggs plus 3 yolks, room temperature
1 cup sugar
$1/2$ cup brown sugar, firmly packed
$3/4$ teaspoon salt
2 teaspoons vanilla extract
$1^1/2$ cups semi-sweet chocolate chips
$1/2$ cup (1 stick) unsalted butter, cold
$1/2$ cup Dutch-process cocoa powder
$1/2$ cup all-purpose flour

Allow time for refrigeration.

1. Preheat oven to 350 degrees F and grease a 9 x 9-inch baking dish or line with parchment paper.
2. To make cookie dough, in a medium bowl, using a rubber spatula, stir together the warm melted butter, sugar, and brown sugar. It will look like wet sand and may not completely come together—that's okay.
3. Stir in the egg and vanilla until smooth.
4. Add in the baking soda, salt, and flour and stir until just combined. Add in the chocolate chips and stir until just incorporated.
5. Reserve about $1/2$ cup of the cookie dough to sprinkle on top of the brownie layer. Transfer the rest of the dough to the prepared baking pan and spread it evenly. Store both in the refrigerator while you make the brownie layer.
6. *If you are just making Chocolate Chip Cookie Bars (and not making the brownie layer), you can stop here.* Press all the dough into the prepared baking pan and bake for 20 to 25 minutes. The bars are done when the edges are very lightly golden brown and the center is evenly and slightly puffed.
7. To make the brownie batter, in the bowl of an electric mixer fitted with a paddle attachment, beat the eggs, yolks, sugar, brown sugar, and salt on medium-high speed until the mixture is light in color and has nearly doubled in volume, 5 to 6 minutes. Turn to a low speed and add the vanilla until just incorporated.
8. While the egg mixture is beating, microwave the chocolate and butter in a heatproof bowl, in 30-second increments, stirring frequently until smooth. Be careful not to scorch the chocolate. Once completely melted, whisk in the cocoa powder until completely combined.
9. Add the warm chocolate-butter mixture to the egg mixture and mix on a low speed until combined. Add the flour and use a rubber spatula to combine.

10. Remove the baking pan with cookie dough from the refrigerator. Pour the brownie batter into the prepared baking pan on top of the cookie dough. Scatter pieces of extra reserved cookie dough over the top of the brownie batter. Press gently on the dough just until it starts to sink down into the batter a little.

11. Bake for 40 to 45 minutes (40 for gooey, 45 or more for fully baked), covering with foil if you need to keep the cookies from getting too brown on top. To check for doneness, insert a toothpick into the center. The toothpick should come out with crumbs, and the batter on the toothpick should not be wet.

12. Transfer the pan to a wire rack and let cool completely. Use the parchment paper to gently lift the brownies from the pan. Cut them into bars and serve.

CHOCOLATE CHIP COOKIE BUTTER BARS

●●●○○ MAKES: 12 TO 14 BARS

Cookie butter is dangerously good. I personally like Biscoff's cookie butter for these bars. Sandwich it between layers of chocolate chip cookie dough, then bake and drizzle with more cookie butter. What do you have? Best. Thing. Ever!

CHOCOLATE CHIP COOKIE BASE

2 cups all-purpose flour

$^1/_2$ teaspoon salt

$^1/_2$ teaspoon baking soda

$^1/_2$ cup (1 stick) unsalted butter, room temperature

1 cup light brown sugar, firmly packed

1 egg, room temperature

1 teaspoon vanilla extract

1 cup mini semi-sweet chocolate chips

COOKIE BUTTER LAYER

$^1/_2$ cup cookie butter (like Biscoff)

$^1/_4$ cup ($^1/_2$ stick) unsalted butter, melted

1 teaspoon vanilla extract

$^1/_2$ teaspoon salt

2 teaspoons milk

$1^1/_2$ cups confectioners' sugar

COOKIE BUTTER DRIZZLE

2 tablespoons cookie butter

CHOCOLATE DRIZZLE

2 tablespoons semi-sweet chocolate chips

2 tablespoons heavy cream

Allow time for refrigeration.

1. Preheat oven to 350 degrees F and grease a 9 x 9-inch baking dish or line with parchment paper.
2. Starting with the cookie base, in a medium bowl, whisk together the flour, salt, and baking soda. Set aside.
3. In the bowl of an electric mixer fitted with a paddle attachment, cream together on a medium speed the butter and brown sugar until well combined. Add the egg and vanilla and mix until combined.
4. Slowly incorporate the dry ingredients and mix until the dough comes together. Mix in the mini chocolate chips.
5. Store the dough in the refrigerator while you prepare the cookie butter layer.
6. In a medium bowl, whisk together the cookie butter and melted butter. Add in the vanilla, salt, and milk until smooth. Switch to a rubber spatula and mix in the confectioners' sugar a half cup at a time until it resembles a dough or paste.
7. Take the cookie dough base out of the refrigerator and firmly pack half the mixture into the bottom of the prepared pan. Make sure it's an even layer and it reaches the edges of the pan.
8. Press the cookie butter dough into an even layer on top of the cookie dough layer. Crumble the other half of the cookie dough on top of the cookie butter layer.
9. Bake for 25 to 30 minutes or until the edges are a light golden brown. Transfer the pan to a wire rack and let cool completely. Let cool completely and use the parchment to lift from the pan.
10. To prepare the cookie butter drizzle, in a small heatproof bowl, microwave the cookie butter for about 30 seconds, stirring until a smooth and pourable consistency.
11. For the chocolate drizzle, in a heatproof bowl, microwave the chocolate chips and heavy cream in 30-second increments, stirring frequently until smooth. Drizzle top of bars with chocolate and cookie butter.
12. Allow to cool; cut into bars and serve.

BROWN BUTTER CHOCOLATE CHIP COOKIE DOOZIES

●●●●○ MAKES: ABOUT 10 SANDWICH COOKIES

Remember those sandwich cookies at the mall when you were a teenager? My favorite version was called Doozies and had two chocolate chip cookies with decadent frosting sandwiched between them. This recipe is an adult version of that cookie. Brown butter gives a nutty, mellow flavor, and the sweet cream cheese frosting has the perfect, complementary, vanilla bean punch.

3/4 cup (1 1/2 sticks) unsalted butter, room temperature

1 1/2 cups all-purpose flour

1 teaspoon baking powder

1/2 teaspoon baking soda

1/2 teaspoon salt

3/4 cup sugar

3/4 cup light brown sugar, firmly packed

1 tablespoon vanilla extract

1 egg plus 1 egg yolk, room temperature

1 1/2 cups semi-sweet chocolate, chopped

CREAM CHEESE BUTTERCREAM

1/2 cup (1 stick) unsalted butter, room temperature

8 ounces cream cheese, room temperature

1 teaspoon vanilla bean paste

1/4 teaspoon salt

4 cups confectioners' sugar

KATIE'S TIP: Cream cheese must be at room temperature for a smooth frosting. This will ensure that the cream cheese whips completely smooth with the other ingredients.

1. Preheat the oven to 350 degrees F and line a large baking sheet with parchment paper or a silicone baking mat.
2. Brown the butter until it reaches an amber color (see page 16 for directions). Let cool to room temperature.
3. In a medium bowl, whisk together the flour, baking powder, baking soda, and salt. Set aside.
4. In another medium bowl, whisk together the cooled brown butter, sugar, brown sugar, and vanilla until incorporated. Add the egg and yolk, and whisk until fully combined, about a minute, until smooth and glossy.
5. Add dry ingredients all at once and use a rubber spatula to mix until just combined. Place the chopped chocolate in the bowl on top of the dough and use your hands to knead it until the chocolate is evenly distributed. The dough will be very shiny, slick, and dense.
6. Using a regular cookie scoop, place 8 or 9 dough balls on the prepared baking sheet, spacing about 3 inches apart.
7. Bake 9 to 11 minutes until edges are golden brown and firm but centers are still soft. Allow to cool on the baking sheet before transferring them to a cooling rack. Continue to bake the rest of the cookie dough.
8. While the cookies cool, make the cream cheese buttercream. In the bowl of an electric mixer fitted with a whisk attachment, beat butter and cream cheese until creamy, well-combined, and lump-free.
9. Add vanilla bean paste and salt and mix well.
10. With mixer on low, gradually add confectioners' sugar until completely combined. Place frosting in a piping bag with large tip.
11. To assemble, pipe some of the filling onto the flat side of half of the cookies. Place the remaining cookies on top to make a sandwich. Serve immediately or store in an airtight container in the refrigerator.

BROWN BUTTER ESPRESSO DARK CHOCOLATE CHIP COOKIES

●●●○○ MAKES: ABOUT 24 COOKIES

I don't mean to be melodramatic, but these cookies are insanely good. The coffee and dark chocolate bring a complex bitterness to the sweet cookie with mellow, nutty brown butter notes before finally being garnished with flaky sea salt. Gourmet and indulgent—could there be a more sophisticated cookie?

$^3/_4$ cup ($1^1/_2$ sticks) unsalted butter, browned and cooled

$1^3/_4$ cups all-purpose flour

$^1/_4$ cup espresso powder

$^1/_2$ teaspoon baking soda

$^1/_2$ teaspoon salt

$^1/_3$ cup sugar

1 cup dark brown sugar, firmly packed

1 egg plus 1 egg yolk, room temperature

2 teaspoons vanilla extract

4 ounces dark chocolate, roughly chopped

4 ounces semi-sweet chocolate, roughly chopped

Flaky sea salt for garnish

Allow time for refrigeration.

1. First brown the butter until it reaches an amber color (see page 16 for directions). Let cool to room temperature.

2. In a medium bowl, whisk together the flour, espresso powder, baking soda, and salt. Set aside.

3. In the bowl of an electric mixer fitted with a paddle attachment, cream together the cooled brown butter, sugar, and brown sugar until smooth. Add in the egg, egg yolk, and vanilla. Mix well, scraping down the bowl as needed.

4. Slowly mix in the dry ingredients until just combined, being careful not to overmix.

5. Remove from the mixer and fold in the chocolate.

6. Line a small, rimmed baking sheet with waxed or parchment paper to chill the dough.

7. Use a regular cookie scoop to scoop the dough, placing balls side by side on the baking sheet. Cover with plastic wrap and place in the refrigerator for at least 4 hours or overnight.

8. When you are ready to bake the cookies, preheat oven to 350 degrees F and line a large baking sheet with parchment paper or a silicone baking mat. Place 5 or 6 dough balls onto the baking sheet, spaced 3 inches apart. Sprinkle the tops of dough balls with flaky sea salt.

9. Bake for 9 to 10 minutes until the edges are just golden brown and the centers have puffed up but are still gooey.

10. Allow them to cool on the baking sheet before transferring them to a cooling rack. Continue to bake the rest of the cookie dough.

KATIE'S TIP: Don't substitute brewed espresso for instant espresso powder here as added liquid will affect the recipe. Instant espresso has a better, darker flavor than your average store-bought instant coffee.

S'MORES CHOCOLATE CHIP COOKIES

●●●○○ MAKES: 12 LARGE COOKIES

My kids (like most) are obsessed with s'mores—always begging their dad to build a bonfire in the backyard so we can roast marshmallows. These chocolate chip cookies are everything s'mores have to offer and more. The browned butter and roasted marshmallows bring that campfire smoky flavor. Graham cracker crumbs mixed in the dough and chunks of Hershey bars make these cookies remarkable—no campfire needed.

1 cup (2 sticks) salted butter, browned and cooled

12 marshmallows

2 1/4 cups all-purpose flour

1 cup graham cracker crumbs (see tip)

1 teaspoon baking soda

1 1/2 teaspoons baking powder

1 teaspoon salt

1 cup dark brown sugar, firmly packed

1/2 cup sugar

2 eggs, room temperature

2 teaspoons vanilla extract

1 cup milk chocolate, chopped (such as Hershey's bars)

1/2 cup broken graham cracker pieces

Garnishes: flaky sea salt, chocolate bar pieces, graham cracker pieces

KATIE'S TIP: For graham cracker crumbs, pulse about 8 graham cracker sheets in a food processor until it resembles a coarse, sandy mixture. If you don't have a food processor, place graham crackers in a zip-top bag, cover with a kitchen towel, and pound with a large kitchen spoon or ladle.

These cookies are best when eaten the same day.

1. Brown the butter until it reaches an amber color (see page 16 for directions). Let cool to room temperature.

2. Preheat oven to 350 degrees F and line a large baking sheet with a silicone baking mat. Spray the baking mat with cooking spray. Place the marshmallows on the baking mat, spacing them out so they won't touch when puffed up. Toast them in the oven for about 5 minutes until the tops are brown/charred (watch them carefully as they burn easily). Take them out of the oven and let cool completely—they will deflate.

3. Line another large baking sheet with parchment paper or a silicone baking mat to prepare for baking cookies.

4. In a medium bowl, whisk together the flour, graham cracker crumbs, baking soda, baking powder, and salt. Set aside.

5. In a separate bowl, whisk together the brown sugar, sugar, and cooled brown butter. Whisk in the eggs and vanilla until smooth.

6. Add the dry ingredients to the butter mixture and fold the batter with a rubber spatula until combined.

7. Stir in the chocolate and graham cracker pieces until just combined.

8. Using a large cookie scoop, fill the scoop half full with dough and then place one of the toasted marshmallows in the center. Fill the rest of the scoop with dough until the marshmallow is covered. Place 6 dough balls onto the baking sheet, spaced 3 inches apart. (Optional: Gently press the extra chocolate bar pieces and graham cracker pieces into the tops of each cookie.)

9. Leave the rest of the dough out at room temperature. Bake cookies for 10 to 14 minutes, until the edges are slightly golden brown but the centers are still soft. Remove from the oven and sprinkle each cookie with flaked sea salt while still hot.

10. Let cool on the baking sheet for at least 5 minutes or until the marshmallows set up before transferring them to a cooling rack. Continue to bake the rest of the cookie dough.

3.

CAKES, PIES, AND GIANT COOKIES

MILK AND CHOCOLATE CHIP COOKIES CAKE

●●●●● MAKES: ONE 8-INCH THREE-LAYER CAKE

This recipe takes the flavors of milk and chocolate chip cookies to create a layer cake perfect for your next family birthday party. It uses "cookie milk," created by steeping chocolate chip cookies in whole milk, in the batter and in the frosting, for a subtle chocolate chip cookie flavor that abounds upon first bite. I love it roughly iced (more like a naked cake) because it's fun to see the chocolate chips shine through the cake—and, oh, that chocolate ganache drip just makes it feel extra special!

COOKIE MILK
2 cups whole milk
10 chocolate chip cookies
   (homemade, store bought, or
   chocolate chip cookie cereal
   on page 169)

CAKE
1 cup (2 sticks) unsalted butter,
   room temperature
1/2 cup vegetable shortening
1 cup sugar
1 cup light brown sugar,
   firmly packed
5 eggs, room temperature
3 cups all-purpose flour
2 teaspoons baking powder
1/2 teaspoon salt
1 cup cookie milk
2 teaspoons vanilla extract
3/4 cup mini chocolate chips
   tossed in 1 tablespoon flour
Chocolate chip cookies for
   garnish, optional

1. Preheat oven to 350 degrees F and butter and flour three 8-inch round cake pans.

TO MAKE THE COOKIE MILK:
2. Pour the whole milk into a medium bowl. Place enough chocolate chip cookies into the milk so the liquid rises just above the cookies. Stir well and steep for 20 to 25 minutes. Strain into a small bowl using a fine-mesh sieve. Gently press the milk out of the cookies using a spatula or wooden spoon. Save 1 cup of the cookie milk for the cake. Save the remainder for the frosting. Discard the soaked cookie crumbs.

TO MAKE THE CAKE:
3. In the bowl of an electric mixer fitted with a paddle attachment, cream together butter and shortening until light and fluffy. Slowly add the sugar and brown sugar one cup at a time, making sure to fully incorporate each cup before adding another. With the mixer on low speed, add the eggs, one at a time, scraping down the bowl after each addition.

4. In a separate bowl, sift together the flour, baking powder, and salt. Pour the cookie milk and vanilla into a large measuring cup and whisk together. In three parts, alternately add the dry ingredients and the milk to the batter, beginning and ending with the dry ingredients. Mix until just combined. Add in mini chocolate chips and mix until just combined.

5. Divide the batter between pans. Bake, rotating the pans halfway through, until golden brown and a toothpick inserted in the center comes out clean, 25 to 35 minutes. Transfer the pans to a wire rack. Once cooled, invert the cakes onto racks; reinvert, top side up. Cool completely. While the cake is cooling, make the frosting.

BUTTERCREAM

1 cup (2 sticks) unsalted butter, room temperature

6 cups confectioners' sugar, divided

1/2 cup cookie milk (leftover from cake recipe)

2 teaspoons vanilla extract

TO MAKE THE BUTTERCREAM:

6. In the bowl of an electric mixer fitted with a whisk attachment, combine the butter, 3 cups of the confectioners' sugar, cookie milk, and vanilla. Beat on medium speed until smooth and creamy, 3 to 5 minutes. Gradually add the remaining confectioners' sugar 1 cup at a time, beating for about 2 minutes after each addition, until the buttercream reaches desired consistency.

7. To assemble the cake, trim the tops of the cake layers if needed. Place one layer of cake onto a cake stand or serving plate. Top with approximately 2/3 cup of buttercream. Repeat with remaining layers and crumb coat the outside, leaving the sides of the cake exposed. Use a bench scraper to smooth out the sides and top of the cake. Chill for at least 20 minutes.

CHOCOLATE GANACHE

1 cup semi-sweet chocolate chips

1/2 cup heavy whipping cream

TO MAKE THE CHOCOLATE GANACHE:

8. Place the chocolate chips in a small heatproof bowl.

9. In a saucepan on medium-low, heat the heavy cream until hot and steaming. Pour the heavy cream on top of the chocolate chips and let it set for 1 minute and 30 seconds. Then, using a rubber spatula, stir until the ganache is smooth and silky.

10. Let cool for 5 minutes. Using a tablespoon, apply the ganache near edges of the cake to create the drips. Pour some ganache on the top of the cake and spread with an offset spatula. Place extra chocolate chip cookies on top of the cake for garnish. Place the cake in the refrigerator for 10 minutes for the ganache to set.

CHOCOLATE CHIP COOKIE SKILLET

●OOOO MAKES: ONE 10-INCH COOKIE SKILLET

Cast iron skillets can be passed down through generations if taken care of properly. I still have my grandmother's and she always taught me to never wash it with soap, to make sure it's perfectly dry before storing, and to rub a little oil into the bottom every couple of uses. I use my skillet to cook just about everything—and I *love* to bake in it. Baking this giant chocolate chip cookie in a skillet makes for crispy edges and bottom with an ultra-gooey center. It's perfect served warm straight from the skillet, topped with vanilla ice cream, with spoons for everyone to dive in.

1 cup (2 sticks) salted butter, room temperature
$^1/_4$ cup sugar
$^3/_4$ cup light brown sugar, firmly packed
2 eggs, room temperature
2 teaspoons vanilla extract
2 cups all-purpose flour
1 teaspoon baking soda
$^1/_2$ teaspoon salt
1 cup semi-sweet chocolate chips
1 cup dark chocolate chips
1 cup semi-sweet chocolate wafers, chopped
Flaky sea salt, for garnish
Vanilla ice cream, optional

1. Preheat the oven to 350 degrees F and lightly butter a 10-inch oven-safe skillet.
2. In a large mixing bowl, using a rubber spatula, beat together the butter, sugar, and brown sugar until smooth. Mix in the eggs, one at a time, until combined. Add the vanilla, beating until creamy. Add the flour, baking soda, and salt. Stir in the chocolate chips and chopped chocolate wafers.
3. Spread the dough into the bottom of the prepared skillet.
4. Transfer the skillet to the oven and bake for 20 to 22 minutes for an extra doughy center or 22 to 25 minutes for a more set cookie. Remove from the oven and let cool for 3 to 5 minutes. Sprinkle with sea salt. Serve warm with vanilla ice cream.
5. **For a S'mores Chocolate Chip Cookie version of this skillet,** you'll need 1 cup semi-sweet chocolate chips, 4 squares graham crackers broken into bite-size pieces, about 20 mini marshmallows, and 3 Hershey's chocolate bars broken into pieces. After you stir in the chocolate chips (you won't need the additional dark chocolate or chocolate wafers from the original recipe), spread $^1/_3$ of the dough into the bottom of the prepared skillet. Arrange the graham crackers over the dough, then add the marshmallows and Hershey's pieces. Add the remaining cookie dough, gently spreading the dough over the marshmallows and chocolate. It's okay if not all the dough covers the marshmallows. Bake per original directions.

CHOCOLATE CHIP COOKIE LAVA CAKES

●●●○○ MAKES: 8 RAMEKINS/MUFFIN CUPS

I posted a ten-second video on Instagram of a spoon scooping the chocolaty center of one of these lava cakes, and it got over 30,000 views. There's just something about a warm chocolate chip cookie with a hidden chocolate lava center that captivates people. Trust me, they're even better in person.

CHOCOLATE GANACHE
1/3 cup heavy cream
2/3 cup semi-sweet chocolate
  chips, chopped

COOKIE DOUGH
1/2 cup (1 stick) unsalted butter,
  room temperature
2 tablespoons sugar
3/4 cup light brown sugar,
  firmly packed
1 egg, room temperature
1 teaspoon baking soda
1/2 teaspoon salt
2 teaspoons vanilla extract
1/4 teaspoon instant espresso
  powder
13/4 cups all-purpose flour
2/3 cup semi-sweet chocolate
  wafers, chopped
Flaky sea salt, for garnish
Vanilla ice cream, optional

Allow time for refrigeration.

TO MAKE THE CHOCOLATE GANACHE:
1. In a small saucepan, bring the heavy cream to a boil.
2. Place the chocolate chips in a medium heatproof bowl and pour the hot cream over the chocolate chips. Let it set for 30 seconds. Then stir until smooth.
3. Place the ganache into the refrigerator for a minimum of 2 hours or until firm and malleable.

TO MAKE THE COOKIE DOUGH:
4. In a medium bowl, using a rubber spatula, cream together the butter, sugar, and brown sugar. Add the egg and beat to combine. Add the baking soda, salt, vanilla, and instant espresso powder and beat until combined. Scrape down the bowl. Gradually add the flour and mix until just combined.
5. Fold in the chocolate chips and chill the dough for at least 30 minutes.
6. To finish the lava cakes, preheat the oven to 350 degrees F and butter eight ramekins/muffin cups.
7. Use a cookie scoop to divide the chocolate ganache mixture into eight portions and keep them ready on a parchment-lined tray.
8. Scoop 1/4-cup-size mounds of the cookie dough (using a 1/4 cup measure or large cookie scoop) and divide into two parts.
9. Flatten one of the parts with your fingertips and place one of the ganache balls on top. Cover with the other cookie dough part and roll into a ball, making sure the ganache is completely covered in cookie dough.
10. You should end up with eight golf-ball-size rounds. Place each round into prepared ramekins. You can bake immediately or store in the refrigerator until ready to bake. You will want to serve them warm from the oven, so bake them when you are ready to serve.
11. Bake for 15 to 17 minutes or until the tops are golden but the lava cakes are still soft to the touch and very slightly jiggly in the center. Sprinkle tops with flaky sea salt.
12. Serve warm with vanilla ice cream.

CHOCOLATE MOCHA PIE WITH ALMOND DARK CHOCOLATE COOKIE CRUST

●●●●○ MAKES: ONE 9-INCH CHEESECAKE

I got the inspiration for this recipe from the Pioneer Woman maybe twenty years ago—back when she was one of the original food bloggers. I love how creative and simple it is to put together. Over the years, I have made it my own, adding a chocolate chip cookie crust that is speckled with dark chocolate and almonds. The filling is silky smooth, created by beating it in a stand mixer for 20 minutes, and rich with chocolate, coffee, and Kahlua.

CHOCOLATE CHIP COOKIE CRUST

1^{1}/$_{2}$ cups all-purpose flour

^{1}/$_{2}$ teaspoon baking soda

^{1}/$_{2}$ teaspoon salt

^{1}/$_{2}$ cup (1 stick) unsalted butter, room temperature

^{1}/$_{2}$ cup light brown sugar, firmly packed

^{1}/$_{4}$ cup sugar

^{1}/$_{2}$ teaspoon vanilla extract

1 egg, room temperature

6 ounces dark chocolate, finely chopped

^{1}/$_{2}$ cup raw slivered almonds, finely chopped

Allow time for refrigeration.

TO MAKE THE CHOCOLATE COOKIE CRUST:

1. Preheat oven to 350 degrees F and spray a 10-inch pie dish with non-stick baking spray.
2. In a medium bowl, whisk together the flour, baking soda, and salt. Set aside.
3. In the bowl of an electric mixer fitted with a paddle attachment, cream together butter, brown sugar, and sugar for 2 minutes until light and fluffy. Add the vanilla and egg. Mix until combined.
4. Slowly add the dry ingredients. Add the chocolate and almonds and mix until combined.
5. Pour the cookie dough into the pie dish. Using your hands and a small piece of plastic wrap, press the cookie dough into the bottom of the pan. The dough should cover the bottom of the pan about a half inch thick.
6. Bake for 18 to 23 minutes until the crust is golden brown. While the crust is still warm, use the bottom of a drinking glass to press down the dough. This deflates any rising that occurred during baking and makes a more compact crust.
7. Allow to cool on a wire rack while you prepare the filling.

FILLING

1 cup (2 sticks) salted butter, room temperature

1 cup sugar

2 teaspoons instant coffee granules

1 teaspoon Kahlua

3 ounces semi-sweet (or bittersweet) chocolate, melted and slightly cooled

1 teaspoon vanilla extract

4 eggs, room temperature

Whipped cream, for garnish

Grated chocolate, for garnish

TO MAKE THE FILLING:

8. In a large bowl of an electric mixer fitted with a whisk attachment, beat the butter, sugar, instant coffee, and Kahlua until fluffy, about 1 to 2 minutes. When the melted chocolate is cooled, drizzle it into the butter mixture as it beats on medium speed. Add the vanilla and beat the mixture until thoroughly combined, scraping down the sides as needed.

9. On medium speed, add the four eggs, one at a time, over a period of 20 minutes. Leave 5 minutes between each egg addition. Scrape down the sides of the bowl halfway through this process. By the end of the fourth egg, the mixture should be silky without any sugar granules. Pour the filling into the pie crust and smooth the top with the back of a rubber spatula.

10. Place the pie in the refrigerator to chill for at least two hours (preferably overnight).

11. Serve with whipped cream and more grated chocolate.

CHOCOLATE CHIP COOKIE LAYER CAKE

●●●○○ MAKES: ONE 7-INCH LAYER COOKIE CAKE

For my chocolate-chip-cookie-loving best friend, Elizabeth, every year on her birthday I make an over-the-top cake. One year it was a brownies and vanilla ice cream layer cake. The next year it was an ice cream sandwich cake. And for a surprise on her thirtieth birthday, I made this chocolate chip cookie layer cake. It is a stunner with giant cookies layered with buttercream. It really is the ultimate birthday cake!

CHOCOLATE CHIP COOKIE CAKE

2^1/4 cups all-purpose flour

^{3}/4 teaspoon baking soda

1 teaspoon salt

1 cup (2 sticks) unsalted butter, room temperature

1 cup light brown sugar, firmly packed

^{1}/2 cup sugar

2 eggs, room temperature

2 teaspoons imitation vanilla

2 cups mini chocolate chips

KATIE'S TIP: You'll need a kitchen scale for this recipe to divide the dough before baking. It ensures that all your cookies will bake to the same size to make the stacked cake.

TO MAKE THE CHOCOLATE CHIP COOKIE CAKE:

1. Start by weighing the bowl from your electric mixer (in grams) in which you are going to mix your cookie dough. Write that number down so you can subtract it from the total weight later to get the true weight of the cookie dough.

2. Preheat oven to 350 degrees F and line a large baking sheet with parchment paper or a silicone baking mat.

3. In a medium bowl, whisk together the flour, baking soda, and salt. Set aside.

4. Using an electric mixer fitted with a paddle attachment, cream together the butter, brown sugar, and sugar on medium speed until light and fluffy. Then mix in the eggs and vanilla.

5. Add the flour mixture and mix until just combined. Remove the bowl from the mixer and use a rubber spatula to fold in the chocolate chips.

6. Weigh the bowl again (in grams) with the cookie dough inside. Subtract the weight of the bowl that you took earlier so you know exactly how much dough you have. Divide that number by 10. This ensures all your cookies are uniform.

7. Place the cookie dough in the refrigerator for about 10 minutes.

8. Weigh out the amount of cookie dough needed for one cookie and place it on your baking sheet. Two cookies should fit on one sheet. Place them about 2 to 3 inches apart.

9. Place another piece of parchment paper on top of your scooped cookie dough. Take something flat and heavy (I use a flat plate) and press down until the chocolate chips stop you from pushing anymore. They'll be about ^{1}/8 inch thick.

10. Bake for 10 to 12 minutes or until the edges are golden brown and the center is set. You'll end up with approximately 7-inch cookies. Take a large spatula and carefully transfer them to a cooling rack. Repeat 4 more times.

Recipe continued on following page.

11. While each batch bakes, place the dough in the refrigerator. You don't want the dough to reach room temperature as it will affect how the cookies bake.
12. Let the cookies cool completely before assembling.

BUTTERCREAM

1 cup (2 sticks) unsalted butter, room temperature
6 cups confectioners' sugar
1 tablespoon vanilla extract
2 to 3 tablespoons milk

TO MAKE THE BUTTERCREAM:

13. In a larger bowl, cream the butter, then slowly mix in the confectioners' sugar one cup at a time. Halfway through, mix in the vanilla and 2 tablespoons of milk.
14. Once all the confectioners' sugar is mixed in, add in another tablespoon of milk if your buttercream is too stiff to spread.
15. To assemble the cake, spread an even layer of buttercream between each cookie. Repeat the process until all 10 layers are stacked, leaving the top of the cake without frosting.
16. Let the cake set out at room temperature, covered, for 4 hours or overnight. This allows the cookies to soften and the buttercream to strengthen the cake.

CHOCOLATE CHIP COOKIE PIE

●●○○○ MAKES: ONE 9-INCH PIE

This is one of those any-occasion pies that is great to have in your recipe arsenal. It would be wonderful served with ice cream for a birthday party and can totally hold its own against pumpkin pie at Thanksgiving. The shortbread crust adds the perfect layer to this gooey pie.

SHORTBREAD CRUST

1 cup (2 sticks) unsalted butter, room temperature
$1/2$ cup confectioners' sugar
2 cups all-purpose flour
1 teaspoon vanilla extract
$1/4$ teaspoon baking powder

CHOCOLATE CHIP COOKIE PIE FILLING

$3/4$ cup ($1^1/2$ sticks) unsalted butter, room temperature
$1/4$ cup sugar
$3/4$ cup light brown sugar, firmly packed
2 eggs, room temperature
1 teaspoon vanilla
$1/8$ teaspoon salt
1 cup all-purpose flour
1 cup semi-sweet chocolate chips

Allow time for refrigeration.

1. Preheat oven to 350 degrees F and lightly butter a 9-inch pie dish.
2. Start by making the shortbread crust. In the bowl of an electric mixer fitted with a paddle attachment, beat the butter on medium speed until fluffy and add the confectioners' sugar.
3. Add the flour and mix until just combined. Add the vanilla and baking powder and mix until mixture is crumbly.
4. Press the dough into the bottom and up the sides of the prepared pie dish. Place the pie crust in the freezer for 15 minutes to help ensure the dough keeps its form up the sides of the pie pan.
5. Bake for 10 minutes until just set but still underdone.
6. Let the crust cool before adding the filling. Turn the oven down to 325 degrees F.
7. While the crust cools, make the chocolate chip cookie pie filling. In the clean bowl of an electric mixer fitted with a paddle attachment, beat the butter, sugar, and brown sugar on medium speed until light and fluffy.
8. Add the eggs and vanilla and mix until well combined.
9. Slowly add the salt and flour and blend on low speed until just combined. Add the chocolate chips and mix until just combined.
10. Pour the batter into the pie crust and bake for 40 to 50 minutes until the pie is golden brown. Do not overbake—it may still look a little underdone in the center, but that's okay.
11. Let the pie cool completely before slicing. The pie will set up as it cools—if you cut into it too early, it will be runny.

PEANUT BUTTER CHOCOLATE CHIP COOKIE PIE

●●●○○ MAKES: ONE 10-INCH PIE

There is something truly nostalgic about a peanut butter pie. It just feels like something Grandma would have made. It has a buttery, sweet, salty filling, is encased in a chocolate chip cookie crust, and is topped with smooth whipped cream—the perfect pie for any time of year.

CHOCOLATE CHIP COOKIE CRUST

1¹/₂ cups all-purpose flour
¹/₂ teaspoon baking soda
¹/₂ teaspoon salt
¹/₂ cup (1 stick) unsalted butter, room temperature
¹/₂ cup light brown sugar, firmly packed
¹/₄ cup sugar
¹/₂ teaspoon vanilla extract
1 egg, room temperature
1 cup mini semi-sweet chocolate chips, plus more for garnish

PEANUT BUTTER FILLING

8 ounces (1 block) cream cheese, room temperature
2 cups confectioners' sugar
3 cups creamy peanut butter
3 cups heavy whipping cream
1 tablespoon, plus 1 teaspoon vanilla extract
Whipped cream, for garnish

Allow time for refrigeration.

TO MAKE THE CHOCOLATE CHIP COOKIE CRUST:

1. Preheat oven to 350 degrees F and spray a 10-inch pie dish with non-stick baking spray.
2. In a medium bowl, whisk together flour, baking soda, and salt. Set aside.
3. In the bowl of an electric mixer fitted with a paddle attachment, cream together the butter, brown sugar, and sugar for 2 minutes until light and fluffy. Add the vanilla and egg. Mix until combined.
4. Slowly add the dry ingredients. Add the chocolate chips and mix until combined.
5. Pour the cookie dough into the pie dish. Using your hands and a small piece of plastic wrap, press the cookie dough into the bottom of the pan. The dough should cover the bottom of the pan about a half inch thick.
6. Bake for 18 to 23 minutes until the crust is golden brown. While the crust is still warm, use the bottom of a drinking glass to press down the dough. This deflates any rising that occurred during baking and makes a more compact crust.
7. Allow to cool on a wire rack while you prepare the filling.

TO MAKE THE PEANUT BUTTER FILLING:

8. In the bowl of an electric mixer fitted with a whisk attachment, beat the cream cheese and confectioners' sugar on high speed until very smooth and creamy, about 2 minutes. Add the peanut butter and beat until combined. Slowly add the 3 cups heavy cream, ¹/₂ cup at a time, until incorporated. Add the vanilla and whip on high speed until light and fluffy, about 1 to 2 minutes. Spoon the peanut butter cream into the cooled crust. Cover and chill 1 hour.
9. Top with fresh whipped cream and sprinkle with the mini chocolate chips when ready to serve.

CHOCOLATE CHIP COOKIE BANANA SNACK CAKE WITH ESPRESSO CREAM CHEESE FROSTING

●●○○○ MAKES: ONE 9 X 13-INCH SHEET CAKE

Sometime in the last couple of years I heard the phrase "snack cake" and thought it was the perfect description for this cake. Baking a cake can seem overwhelming with fussy layers and intricate decorations, but this sheet cake is anything but. This simple recipe produces a dense, moist texture (like carrot cake or banana bread) and is topped with a cream cheese frosting spiked with espresso powder. Store in the refrigerator so it'll be ready for serving to company or, more importantly, for snacking.

2 cups all-purpose flour

1 teaspoon baking soda

1/2 teaspoon cinnamon

1/2 teaspoon salt

1/2 cup (1 stick) unsalted butter, room temperature

3/4 cup sugar

3/4 cup light brown sugar, firmly packed

2 eggs, room temperature

1 teaspoon vanilla extract

3 large bananas, mashed

1/2 cup plain Greek yogurt

1 cup semi-sweet chocolate chips, or chopped chocolate bar of choice

ESPRESSO CREAM CHEESE FROSTING

8 ounces (1 block) cream cheese

1/2 cup (1 stick) unsalted butter

1 tablespoon instant espresso powder

2 1/2 cups confectioners' sugar

1 teaspoon vanilla extract

Allow time for freezing.

1. Preheat the oven to 325 degrees F and grease a 9 x 13-inch baking pan or line with parchment paper.
2. In a small bowl, whisk together the flour, baking soda, cinnamon, and salt. Set aside.
3. In the bowl of your electric mixer fitted with a paddle attachment, beat together the butter, sugar, and brown sugar on medium speed until light and fluffy, about 5 minutes. Beat in the eggs one at a time, scraping down the bowl as needed. Add the vanilla, mashed bananas, and yogurt and mix until well combined and there are no streaks of yogurt.
4. Stir in the dry ingredients on low speed, scraping down the sides if needed, until just combined, being careful not to overmix.
5. Pour the mixture into the greased baking dish. Bake for 25 to 30 minutes, or until a tester inserted in the center comes out clean. Remove from the oven and immediately place pan directly into the freezer. This will make the cake very moist and dense.
6. While the cake is cooling, make the cream cheese frosting.

TO MAKE THE ESPRESSO CREAM CHEESE FROSTING:

7. Beat the cream cheese and butter together until creamy. Beat in the espresso powder until the granules dissolve into the butter mixture. Beat in the confectioners' sugar one cup at a time, scraping down the bowl as needed. Beat in the vanilla until combined and glassy.
8. Pour the frosting on top of the cooled cake and use an offset spatula to spread it evenly. Garnish the top of the cake with extra chocolate chips or chopped chocolate bar.
9. Cover and store in the refrigerator.

CHOCOLATE CHIP COOKIE CAKE

●●●○○ MAKES: ONE 11-INCH COOKIE CAKE

When I first married my husband, he insisted on a cookie cake from the mall. I offered to make him a different kind of cake, but nope; it had to be a cookie cake. Now that I've created the ultimate cookie cake recipe, I get the satisfaction of baking his birthday cake, and he gets his favorite— without a trip to the mall!

1 cup semi-sweet chocolate chips, divided

1/2 cup (1 stick) unsalted butter, melted

1/2 cup light brown sugar, firmly packed

1/4 cup sugar

1 egg, room temperature

2 teaspoons vanilla extract

1/2 teaspoon baking soda

1/4 teaspoon baking powder

1/4 teaspoon salt

1 1/2 cups all-purpose flour

BUTTERCREAM FROSTING

1 cup (2 sticks) unsalted butter, room temperature

1 cup shortening

6 cups confectioners' sugar

2 teaspoons vanilla extract

4 tablespoons milk

3/4 cup chocolate chips, melted and cooled

1. Preheat oven to 350 degrees F and grease an 11-inch round baking pan.
2. Place 1/2 cup of the chocolate chips in a plastic bag and use a rolling pin to break them down into small pieces (leaving 1/2 cup chocolate chips unbroken). Set aside.
3. Place the melted butter in a large bowl and add the brown sugar and sugar. Using a rubber spatula, stir until combined. Add the egg and vanilla, then mix.
4. Next, add the baking soda, baking powder, and salt and mix again. Add the flour and mix until the flour disappears into the dough.
5. Add the 1/2 cup of chopped chocolate chips and the 1/2 cup of whole chocolate chips to the dough and mix. Dump the dough into the prepared pan and use your hands to press it all the way to the sides, smoothing out the top (it will make a very thin layer). Make sure the chocolate chips are well dispersed throughout the dough.
6. Bake for 12 to 14 minutes until just set, being careful not to overbake. You want the cookie cake to be slightly brown on the top and look slightly underbaked. Remove from the oven and place the entire pan on a cooling rack. Allow to cool completely before removing.
7. Once cooled, use a knife to go around the edges, place a flat platter on top, then flip the pan over to remove. After flipping over the cookie cake, flip it over again on the final plate or platter.

TO MAKE THE BUTTERCREAM FROSTING:

8. In the bowl of an electric mixer fitted with a whisk attachment, beat the softened butter and shortening on medium-high speed for 2 minutes until smooth. Turn the mixer to low speed, then add the confectioners' sugar 1/2 cup at a time, stopping and scraping down the sides as needed. Add the vanilla and turn the mixer to medium speed. Add the milk one tablespoon at a time. Beat on high speed for 2 to 3 minutes until creamy and the frosting is at a good consistency to pipe. Transfer half of the buttercream to a piping bag and set aside. To the remaining buttercream, add the melted (room temperature) chocolate and beat on medium-high speed until fully incorporated. Transfer to another piping bag fitted with desired piping tips and pipe the desired design on the top of the cookie cake.

CHOCOLATE CHIP COOKIE CREAM CHEESE POUND CAKE

●●○○○ MAKES: ONE 10-INCH BUNDT CAKE

Don't underestimate a pound cake. My mom's cream cheese pound cake has been a staple in our family for as long as I can remember. It even made it into my first book! I took that tried-and-true recipe and added a chocolate chip cookie twist—with brown sugar, chocolate chips, and the most delicious brown sugar glaze.

POUND CAKE

1 1/2 cups (3 sticks) unsalted
   butter, room temperature
8 ounces (1 block) cream cheese,
   room temperature
2 cups sugar
1 cup light brown sugar,
   firmly packed
6 eggs, room temperature
1 teaspoon salt
1/4 cup buttermilk
2 teaspoons vanilla extract
1 teaspoon almond extract
3 cups all-purpose flour
1 cup mini chocolate chips
1 cup semi-sweet chocolate chips

BROWN SUGAR GLAZE

1/4 cup (1/2 stick) salted butter
1/2 cup light brown sugar,
   firmly packed
2 tablespoons milk
1/4 teaspoon vanilla
1/2 cup confectioners' sugar
Mini chocolate chips for garnish

1. Preheat the oven to 325 degrees F and grease and flour a 10-inch bundt pan.
2. In an electric mixture fitted with a paddle attachment, cream the butter and cream cheese on medium speed until smooth. Add the sugar and brown sugar gradually, beating until fluffy. Add the eggs, one at a time, beating well after each. Add the salt, buttermilk, vanilla, and almond extract, and blend until smooth. Add the flour and chocolate chips all at one time and mix until just incorporated.
3. Pour into the prepared pan. Bake for 1 hour and 20 minutes or until a wooden toothpick inserted into the center of the cake comes out clean. Cool in the pan for 10 minutes and then invert onto a serving plate.
4. While cake is cooling, prepare the brown sugar glaze.

TO MAKE THE BROWN SUGAR GLAZE:

5. Combine the butter, brown sugar, and milk in a saucepan. Bring to a simmer and cook until the sugar dissolves, 1 to 2 minutes.
6. Remove from the heat and let cool 5 minutes.
7. Stir in the vanilla. Add the confectioners' sugar 1/4 cup at a time.
8. Drizzle over the cake. Garnish with more chocolate chips.

CHOCOLATE CHIP COOKIE CUPCAKES

●●●●○ MAKES: ABOUT 3 DOZEN CUPCAKES

My oldest, Emmaline, always wants to bake cupcakes, and lately I've had a lot of chocolate chip cookie dough on hand. *Ha!* I thought, *What if I just baked a cookie right into the center of a cupcake?* This turned out to be a beautiful, basic vanilla cupcake recipe with a chocolate chip cookie baked into the bottom, topped with my favorite vanilla buttercream, and of course garnished with chocolate chip cookies, making the cutest cupcake topper.

MINI CHOCOLATE CHIP COOKIES
See page 31 for ingredients

CUPCAKES
1¹/2 cups all-purpose flour
1¹/2 cups cake flour
  (not self-rising)
1 tablespoon baking powder
¹/2 teaspoon salt
1 cup (2 sticks) unsalted butter,
  room temperature
1³/4 cups sugar
4 eggs, room temperature
2 teaspoons vanilla extract
1¹/4 cups whole milk

BUTTERCREAM FROSTING
1 cup (2 sticks) unsalted butter,
  room temperature
6 to 8 cups confectioners' sugar
¹/2 cup milk
2 teaspoons vanilla extract

TO MAKE THE COOKIES:
1. Make the Mini Chocolate Chip Cookies from page 31 for the perfect cupcake garnish. Only bake half of the cookie dough though. Reserve the other half of dough to bake into the bottom of the cupcakes.

TO MAKE THE CUPCAKES:
2. Line three 12-cup muffin tins with baking cups. In a medium bowl, whisk together flour, cake flour, baking powder, and salt. Set aside.
3. In the bowl of an electric mixer fitted with a paddle attachment, beat the butter and sugar on medium speed until pale and fluffy, about 3 minutes. Reduce speed to low. Add the eggs, one at a time, then the vanilla. Beat in the flour mixture in three additions, alternating with the milk, beginning and ending with the flour mixture.
4. Press 1 tablespoon of the cookie dough into the bottom of each baking cup. Top each with 2 tablespoons batter. Bake for 18 to 20 minutes, until a toothpick inserted into the centers comes out clean. Transfer the tins to cooling racks; let stand for 5 minutes. Transfer the cupcakes to cooling racks. Let cool completely. Continue with the rest of the cupcake batter.

TO MAKE THE BUTTERCREAM FROSTING:
5. In the bowl of an electric mixer fitted with a whisk attachment, beat the butter, 4 cups of the confectioners' sugar, milk, and vanilla on medium speed until smooth and creamy, about 3 to 5 minutes. Gradually add the remaining confectioners' sugar, one cup at a time, beating well after each addition (about 2 minutes), until the icing is thick and a good spreading consistency.
6. Transfer the frosting to a pastry bag fitted with a star tip. Pipe the frosting onto the cupcakes, and top each with a cookie and mini chocolate chips.

KATIE'S TIP: To pipe a cupcake in one large swirl, start your swirl on the outside of the cupcake. Create an outer circle, applying even pressure to the piping bag as you go. Once you've reached the starting point of the outer swirl, start piping the inner swirl so that you overlap the outer swirl a bit. The peak of the swirl should sit on top of the inner swirl. Give one last little squeeze to create the peak, then release the pressure on the piping bag as you pull up.

CHOCOLATE CHIP COOKIE DOUGH CHEESECAKE

●●●●● MAKES: ONE 9-INCH CHEESECAKE

This showstopping cheesecake has a chocolate chip cookie crust and edible cookie dough balls baked into the cheesecake. I'll be honest, it is a labor-intensive recipe with multiple steps, a water bath, cooling time, and frozen dough, but don't let that deter you. This recipe is an adventure worth having, and this cheesecake is a dessert worth sharing.

CHOCOLATE CHIP COOKIE CRUST

1¹/2 cups all-purpose flour
¹/2 teaspoon baking soda
¹/2 teaspoon salt
¹/2 cup (1 stick) unsalted butter, room temperature
¹/2 cup light brown sugar, firmly packed
¹/4 cup sugar
¹/2 teaspoon vanilla extract
1 egg, room temperature
1 cup semi-sweet chocolate chips

EDIBLE COOKIE DOUGH

1¹/2 cups all-purpose flour, heat-treated (see directions on page 21)
¹/4 teaspoon salt
¹/2 cup (1 stick) unsalted butter, room temperature
¹/2 cup light brown sugar, firmly packed
¹/2 cup sugar
1 teaspoon vanilla extract
3 tablespoons whole milk
¹/2 cup semi-sweet chocolate chips
¹/2 cup mini chocolate chips

Allow time for freezing and refrigeration.

TO MAKE THE CHOCOLATE CHIP COOKIE CRUST:

1. Preheat oven to 350 degrees F and spray a 9-inch springform pan with non-stick baking spray.
2. In a medium bowl, whisk together the flour, baking soda, and salt. Set aside.
3. In the bowl of an electric mixer fitted with a paddle attachment, cream together the butter, brown sugar, and sugar for 2 minutes, until light and fluffy. Add the vanilla and egg. Mix until combined.
4. Slowly add the dry ingredients. Add the chocolate chips and mix until combined.
5. Pour all of the cookie dough into the pan. Using your hands and a small piece of plastic wrap, press the cookie dough into the bottom of the pan.
6. Bake for 18 to 23 minutes until the crust is golden brown. While the crust is still warm, use the bottom of a drinking glass to press down the dough. This deflates any rising that occurred during baking and makes a more compact crust.
7. Allow to cool on a wire rack while you prepare the edible cookie dough.

TO MAKE THE EDIBLE COOKIE DOUGH:

8. In a medium bowl, whisk together the flour and salt. Set aside.
9. In the bowl of an electric mixer fitted with a paddle attachment, beat the butter, brown sugar, and sugar together for 2 minutes on medium until light and fluffy. Add the vanilla and milk and mix to combine.
10. Slowly add the dry ingredients, scraping the bowl once combined. Then add both types of chocolate chips. Mix again until combined.
11. Line a small baking sheet with parchment paper or a silicone baking mat. Take a tiny amount of dough and roll it into a ball about the size of a blueberry. Continue making small balls until you have used

Recipe continued on following page.

up all the dough and filled the cookie sheet with tiny cookie dough balls. They do not need to be placed neatly on the pan.

12. Place baking sheet with cookie dough balls in the freezer until very firm, at least 15 minutes, or until ready to add into the cheesecake.

CHEESECAKE
24 ounces cream cheese
   (3 blocks), room temperature
3/4 cup sugar
1 teaspoon vanilla bean paste
1/2 cup sour cream, room
   temperature
1/4 cup heavy whipping cream,
   room temperature
3 eggs, room temperature
2/3 cookie dough balls

TO MAKE THE CHEESECAKE:

13. Once the cookie crust is done baking, allow it to slightly cool while making the cheesecake batter.

14. In the bowl of an electric mixer fitted with a whisk attachment, beat the cream cheese on high for 1 minute until fluffy. Scrape down the bowl and add the sugar and beat again on high for 1 minute. Scrape the bowl. There should be no large chunks of cream cheese left.

15. Add the vanilla bean paste, sour cream, and heavy cream. Mix on low until combined, then turn to medium-high and beat for 30 seconds. It should be creamy with no chunks of cream cheese. Scrape the bowl, and if there are cream cheese chunks, beat again for 30 seconds.

16. Add the eggs one at a time while mixing on low speed. Mix until just combined. Scrape the bowl one more time and mix for 10 more seconds. Using a rubber spatula, fold in two-thirds of the frozen cookie dough balls. Since they are frozen, they will remain as cookie dough as they bake.

17. Pour the batter into the springform pan with the cookie crust. Cover the bottom of the pan completely twice with aluminum foil, making sure water can't penetrate into the cheesecake during the water bath. Then, fill a roasting pan with hot water and place the springform pan in the water so the water reaches about halfway up the cake pan.

18. Bake for 75 to 90 minutes. The cheesecake should be light golden brown on the edges with no cracks. The cheesecake is done baking when there is a slight jiggle in the middle and the edges are set. Prop oven door open and turn off the oven. Let the cheesecake slowly cool in the oven for 30 minutes.

19. Take the cheesecake out of the water bath and transfer to a cooling rack. Allow the cheesecake to cool completely before wrapping in aluminum foil and storing in the refrigerator for at least 6 hours or overnight.

20. Remove the cheesecake from the refrigerator. Remove the pan collar by unhooking the hinge. Slide the cake off the bottom of the pan onto a serving dish.

CHOCOLATE GANACHE

1 cup semi-sweet chocolate chips
1/2 cup heavy whipping cream

WHIPPED CREAM

1 cup heavy whipping cream,
  cold
2 tablespoons confectioners'
  sugar
1/2 teaspoon vanilla extract

TO MAKE THE CHOCOLATE GANACHE:

21. Place the chocolate chips in a small heatproof bowl. Take the cookie dough balls out of the freezer and place on the counter.
22. In a saucepan on medium-low, heat the heavy cream until hot and steaming. Pour heavy cream on top of chocolate chips and let it sit for 1 minute and 30 seconds. Then, using a rubber spatula, stir until ganache is smooth and silky.
23. Let cool for 5 minutes and then pour the ganache into the middle of the cheesecake. Use an offset spatula to smooth the ganache. Place in the refrigerator for 10 minutes for the ganache to set.

TO MAKE THE WHIPPED CREAM:

24. While the ganache is chilling, make the whipped cream.
25. In the clean bowl of an electric mixer fitted with a whisk attachment, beat the cold heavy cream, confectioners' sugar, and vanilla on high until stiff peaks form.
26. Pipe whipped cream on the cheesecake. Top with cookie dough balls and mini chocolate chips.
27. Serve immediately or store in the refrigerator.

KATIE'S TIP: Raw flour should be treated before consuming. Place flour on a rimmed baking sheet and bake for 5 minutes to kill any salmonella. Let cool completely before using in recipe.

CHOCOLATE CHIP COOKIE DOUGH LAYER CAKE

●●●●● MAKES: ONE 8-INCH THREE-LAYER CAKE

We've reached the mecca. The climax of this book must be this cake. It is decadent, beautiful, and a showstopper. It has disks of cookie dough baked right into a fluffy vanilla cake, layered with buttercream, topped with chocolate ganache, and then more cookie dough. This is the ultimate cake for any celebration.

COOKIE DOUGH
1/2 cup (1 stick) unsalted butter, room temperature
1/2 cup sugar
2/3 cup light brown sugar, firmly packed
1/4 cup whole milk
2 teaspoons vanilla extract
2 cups all-purpose flour, heat-treated (see directions on page 21)
1/2 teaspoon salt
1 cup mini chocolate chips

CAKE
3 cups all-purpose flour
2 teaspoons baking powder
1 teaspoon salt
1 cup whole milk
2 teaspoons vanilla extract
1 1/2 cups (3 sticks) unsalted butter, room temperature
2 cups sugar
3 eggs, room temperature
1/2 cup sour cream
1 cup mini chocolate chips

Allow time for refrigeration.

TO MAKE THE COOKIE DOUGH:
1. In the bowl of an electric mixer fitted with a paddle attachment, cream the butter, sugar, and brown sugar together on medium speed.
2. Add the milk and vanilla and mix until combined.
3. Add the flour and salt all at once and mix until just combined. Add the mini chocolate chips and mix until incorporated.
4. Use a small cookie scoop to scoop 18 dough balls and then flatten them slightly. Place the flattened cookie dough balls in an airtight container lined with waxed paper and put in the refrigerator along with the leftover dough.

TO MAKE THE CAKE:
5. Preheat the oven to 350 degrees F and prepare three 8-inch round cake pans. Coat them with non-stick spray and cut out 3 rounds of parchment paper to fit in the bottom of each pan.
6. In a medium bowl, whisk together the flour, baking powder, and salt. Set aside.
7. In a measuring glass, pour in the milk and whisk in the vanilla. Set aside.
8. In the bowl of an electric mixer fitted with a whisk attachment, cream the butter and sugar together on medium speed until light and fluffy (3 to 5 minutes).
9. Keep the speed on medium and mix in the eggs, one at a time, making sure each egg is fully incorporated before adding the next. Mix in the sour cream.
10. Add the flour and milk mixtures, alternating between the two by starting and ending with the flour mixture. This will be three additions of the flour mixture and two of the milk.
11. Lastly, remove the bowl from the mixer and use a rubber spatula to fold in the mini chocolate chips.

Recipe continued on following page.

12. Divide the batter evenly among the cake pans and spread it evenly.
13. Remove the flattened cookie dough balls from the refrigerator and push down 5 cookie dough "disks" in each cake pan. Spread the batter over the top of the cookie dough so that you can no longer see any dough.
14. Bake for 30 to 35 minutes or until a toothpick in the center comes out clean. You may need to rotate the cakes halfway through to ensure they bake evenly.
15. Let the cakes cool in the pans for about 20 minutes. Then run a knife around the inside of the pans and turn the cakes out onto a cooling rack. Peel the paper off the bottoms.
16. Let the cakes cool completely before frosting.

COOKIE DOUGH BUTTERCREAM

$1^{1}/2$ cups (3 sticks) unsalted butter, room temperature
$3/4$ cup light brown sugar, firmly packed
1 cup all-purpose flour
4 cups confectioners' sugar
$1/4$ cup whole milk
2 teaspoons vanilla extract
$1/2$ teaspoon salt
$1/2$ cup mini chocolate chips

TO MAKE THE COOKIE DOUGH BUTTERCREAM:

17. In the bowl of an electric mixer fitted with a whisk attachment, cream together the butter and brown sugar on medium speed.
18. Gradually mix in the flour and confectioners' sugar 2 cups at a time. Pour in the milk between each addition.
19. Lastly, mix in the vanilla and salt.
20. To assemble the cake, spread an even layer of buttercream between each cake layer. Each layer uses one large heaping scoop, using a standard-sized rubber spatula.
21. Once the cake layers are stacked, pop the naked cake in the fridge for about 20 minutes. This helps the layers set so the cake doesn't slide when you frost the outside.
22. Now add the $1/2$ cup of mini chocolate chips to what's left of the buttercream. After 20 minutes, apply an even layer of the cookie dough buttercream to the outside of the cake.
23. Place the cake back in the refrigerator while you prepare the ganache.

CHOCOLATE GANACHE

4 ounces bittersweet chocolate, chopped
$1/2$ cup heavy cream
2 to 3 teaspoons vegetable oil

TO MAKE THE CHOCOLATE GANACHE:

24. Measure out the chocolate in a bowl and set aside.
25. Pour the heavy cream into a glass measuring cup and heat in the microwave for 1 minute or until it starts to bubble.
26. Pour the hot cream over the chopped chocolate and whisk until smooth. To thin it out for the cake drip, add 2 to 3 teaspoons of oil. To test and see if it's the right consistency, lift your whisk out of the ganache and watch how it drips back into the bowl. If it runs back into the bowl in a smooth stream, it's ready to go. If it's still too thick, add another teaspoon of oil.
27. Immediately pour the ganache in the center of the cake and use a small offset spatula to push the ganache toward the sides, allowing it to drip down.
28. Garnish the top of the cake by crumbling the remaining cookie dough that's left in the fridge over the top of the cake.

CHOCOLATE MOUSSE PIE WITH CHOCOLATE CHIP COOKIE CRUST AND MASCARPONE WHIPPED CREAM

●●●●● MAKES: ONE 9-INCH PIE

This pie is *next level*. Now, I must be honest with you: it's time-consuming, but you won't regret making it. It's a showstopper. It has a thick chocolate chip cookie crust, a cool chocolate filling, and a creamy mascarpone whipped cream topping. I've made it alongside a pumpkin pie for Thanksgiving, for friends at a dinner party, and with birthday candles for my husband's birthday. It. Is. All. The. Things.

CHOCOLATE CHIP COOKIE CRUST

1 cup (2 sticks) butter, room temperature

3/4 cup sugar

1 cup light brown sugar, firmly packed

2 eggs, room temperature

2 teaspoons vanilla extract

4 cups all-purpose flour

1/4 teaspoon baking soda

1 1/4 teaspoons salt

1 cup mini chocolate chips

Allow time for refrigeration.

TO MAKE THE CHOCOLATE CHIP COOKIE CRUST:

1. Grease the inside of a 9-inch springform pan and the outside of a cake pan that fits inside the springform pan, leaving a quarter-inch gap all the way around the sides.
2. In the bowl of an electric mixer fitted with a paddle attachment, cream together the butter, sugar, and brown sugar until light and fluffy. Scrape down the bowl.
3. Mix in the eggs and vanilla, until just combined.
4. In a separate bowl, whisk together the flour, baking soda, and salt.
5. Slowly add the dry ingredients to the butter mixture and mix until just combined, being careful not to overmix. Stir in the mini chocolate chips. The dough will be thick and stiff.
6. Pack the cookie dough into the springform pan, pressing the dough up the sides of the pan. The bottom should be about 1 inch thick and the sides 1/4 inch thick. Place a round, cut piece of parchment in the center on top of the dough and press the greased cake pan into the center of the springform pan. Some cookie dough may push up and out of the mold. Leave the cake pan in place and scrape the excess cookie dough away.
7. Refrigerate the pan of dough for at least two hours.
8. Preheat oven to 350 degrees F and place the springform pan on a baking sheet to catch any spillover. Bake for 30 to 35 minutes. Halfway through the baking time, use an oven mitt and push the cake pan down again. Cookie dough will expand out of the mold as it bakes, but you can remove the excess later.

Recipe continued on following page.

9. Remove from the oven when cookie dough crust is nice and golden brown. Let cool completely before removing the cake pan. Once the crust is cool, twist the cake pan and carefully lift it out of the springform pan. Leave the crust inside the springform pan and set aside while you prepare the mousse.

CHOCOLATE MOUSSE

2^1/2 cups heavy cream, divided
5 egg yolks, room temperature
^{1}/2 cup sugar
^{1}/4 teaspoon salt
1 teaspoon vanilla extract
10 ounces semi-sweet chocolate, finely chopped

TO MAKE THE CHOCOLATE MOUSSE:

10. Heat 1 cup of the heavy cream in a small, heavy saucepan until just hot.
11. In a medium saucepan off the heat, whisk the egg yolks. Whisking constantly, slowly add the sugar to the egg yolks, then the salt, and then slowly pour in the warmed heavy cream. Cook over medium heat, stirring constantly, until the mixture thickens and coats the back of a spoon (the custard will thicken as it cools). Pour the mixture through a fine-mesh sieve into a large bowl and stir in the vanilla.
12. In a heatproof bowl, microwave the chocolate in 30-second increments, stirring frequently until smooth. Whisk the chocolate into the mousse until smooth, then let cool.
13. In the bowl of a stand mixer fitted with a whisk attachment, beat the remaining 1^1/2 cups of heavy cream until stiff peaks form. Whisk one-third of the whipped cream into the chocolate mousse to lighten it, then gently fold in the remaining whipped cream. Transfer the mousse to the chocolate chip cookie crust in the springform pan. Use an offset spatula to spread it in an even layer. Chill the pie uncovered for at least 4 hours.

MASCARPONE WHIPPED CREAM

^{3}/4 cup mascarpone cheese
^{1}/3 cup sugar
Pinch of salt
1 cup heavy cream
2 teaspoons vanilla extract

TO MAKE THE MASCARPONE WHIPPED CREAM:

14. In the bowl of a stand mixer fitted with a whisk attachment, beat together the mascarpone cheese, sugar, and salt on low speed until combined. Increase the speed to medium and beat until light, 2 to 3 minutes. On low speed, slowly add half the cream until combined, then stop the mixer and scrape down the sides of the bowl, making sure the cheese is completely combined into the cream. Add the rest of the cream and the vanilla on low speed. Increase the speed to medium-high and beat until the cream is smooth and thick. When the pie is set, top with the whipped cream.
15. Garnish the top of the pie with chocolate shavings and mini chocolate chips. Store the pie in the refrigerator.

FROZEN CHOCOLATE CHIP COOKIE DOUGH CHEESECAKE

●●●○○ MAKES: ONE 9-INCH CHEESECAKE

One of our holiday family traditions is to make a Frozen Peppermint Cheesecake. It's festive and delicious, but the thing I really like about it is that it's easy to make ahead and store in the freezer until our Christmas dinner. The same holds true for this frozen chocolate chip cookie dough version. Make it ahead of time and save the mess and the fuss before an evening of entertaining.

CHOCOLATE CHIP COOKIE CRUST

1¹/2 cups all-purpose flour
¹/2 teaspoon baking soda
¹/2 teaspoon salt
¹/2 cup (1 stick) unsalted butter, room temperature
¹/2 cup light brown sugar, firmly packed
¹/4 cup sugar
¹/2 teaspoon vanilla extract
1 egg, room temperature
1 cup semi-sweet chocolate chips

EDIBLE COOKIE DOUGH
(See recipe on page 143)

CHEESECAKE FILLING
8 ounces (1 block) cream cheese, room temperature
1 (14 ounce) can sweetened condensed milk
2 cups whipping cream, whipped
Whipped cream for garnish

Allow time for overnight freezing.

TO MAKE THE CHOCOLATE CHIP COOKIE CRUST:

1. Preheat oven to 350 degrees F and spray a 9-inch springform pan with non-stick baking spray.
2. In a medium bowl, whisk together the flour, baking soda, and salt. Set aside.
3. In the bowl of an electric mixer fitted with a paddle attachment, cream together the butter, brown sugar, and sugar for 2 minutes until light and fluffy. Add in the vanilla and egg. Mix until combined.
4. Slowly add in the dry ingredients. Add the chocolate chips and mix until combined.
5. Pour the cookie dough into the pan. Using your hands and a small piece of plastic wrap, press the dough into the bottom of the pan.
6. Bake for 18 to 23 minutes until the crust is golden brown. While the crust is still warm, use the bottom of a drinking glass to press down the dough to deflate any rising that occurred during baking.
7. Allow to cool on a wire rack while you prepare the filling.
8. Meanwhile, make the edible cookie dough from page 143.

TO MAKE THE CHEESECAKE FILLING:

9. In the bowl of an electric mixer fitted with a whisk attachment, beat the cream cheese on a high speed until fluffy. Add the sweetened condensed milk and mix well. Remove the bowl from the mixer. Using a rubber spatula, fold in the whipped cream until just combined, then fold in the frozen cookie dough balls, reserving a handful for garnish. Pour into the cooled crust. Freeze, covered, until set (at least 24 hours).
10. Before serving, allow the cheesecake to set at room temperature about 10 minutes to make it easier to slice. Unlatch the springform pan and top with whipped cream and the reserved cookie dough balls.

CHOCOLATE CHIP COOKIE ICEBOX CAKE

●●○○○ MAKES: ONE 9-INCH CAKE

Icebox cakes are a fun, old-fashioned treat that are due for a comeback. When cookies are layered with mascarpone whipped cream and stored in the refrigerator, a little magic happens. The cookies soften and meld into the cream, creating an indescribable texture that is soft and firm all at the same time. This icebox cake is cool and creamy and a great make-ahead treat. Try the classic version or check out the little additional recipe at the end that adds Nutella, Kahlua, and coffee—taking this cake to the next level, from *wow* to *wowzer*!

16 ounces mascarpone, room
   temperature
$^2/_3$ cup, plus 3 tablespoons sugar,
   divided
$2^1/_2$ teaspoons vanilla extract
3 cups whipping cream,
   plus more for topping
16 chocolate chip cookies (see
   Classic Chocolate Chip Cookie
   recipe on page 28)
Mini chocolate chips for garnish

KATIE'S TIP: This recipe calls for a springform pan, but if you don't have one, don't be discouraged! Make a more free-formed cake directly on a serving platter: arrange 7 cookies in a circle on a cake stand or a plate, placing 2 cookies in the center. Carefully spread 1 cup of the cream mixture evenly over the cookies, leaving a $^1/_4$-inch border. Be gentle when spreading as you want to try to keep the cookies together in their circle. Repeat with 7 more cookies and cream, to create four layers total, ending with a layer of cream.

Allow time for refrigeration.

1. In the bowl of an electric mixer fitted with a whisk attachment, cream together on medium speed the mascarpone, $^2/_3$ cup of the sugar, and vanilla until smooth and well combined. Set aside.

2. In the clean bowl of an electric mixer fitted with a whisk attachment, whisk together the whipping cream and remaining 3 tablespoons of sugar on medium speed until stiff peaks just form. Remove the bowl from the mixer and use a rubber spatula to fold the mascarpone mixture into the whipped cream.

3. To assemble the cake, spread a very thin layer of mascarpone whipped cream onto the surface of a 9-inch springform pan and top with a single layer of cookies, breaking up a couple of cookies and fitting the pieces into the larger gaps if needed.

4. Top the cookies with another layer of whipped cream and repeat with cookies and more whipped cream until all the cookies have been used (about 3 layers).

5. Refrigerate the icebox cake for at least 12 hours, or overnight.

6. Remove from the refrigerator and unmold from the springform pan. Top the cake with whipped cream and extra chocolate chips. Slice and serve immediately.

7. **For a Mocha Nutella version of this cake**, add $^3/_4$ cup of Nutella to the mascarpone and whip as directed. To the whipped cream, beat in $^1/_4$ cup Kahlua and 1 teaspoon instant espresso powder after soft peaks have formed. Layer the cake as directed.

CHOCOLATE CHIP COOKIE ICE CREAM CAKE

●●●○○ MAKES: ONE 9-INCH ROUND CAKE

I don't think it matters how old you are—ice cream cake will always be exciting. I make this chocolate chip cookie ice cream cake for kids' birthday parties, Father's Day, dinner parties, you name it. This recipe takes store-bought ice cream cake to the next level with homemade chocolate chip cookies, chocolate ganache, and fresh whipped cream.

ICE CREAM CAKE

9 to 12 chocolate chip cookies (see Classic Chocolate Chip Cookie recipe on page 28)

1/4 cup (1/2 stick) unsalted butter, melted and cooled

1 quart ice cream, flavor of choice (like cookie dough or vanilla)

Mini chocolate chips for garnish

Extra chocolate chip cookies for garnish

CHOCOLATE GANACHE

2/3 cup semi-sweet chocolate chips

1/2 cup heavy whipping cream

WHIPPED CREAM

1 cup heavy whipping cream

2 tablespoons confectioners' sugar

1/2 teaspoon vanilla extract

KATIE'S TIP: Add your favorite ice cream flavor to this recipe. Cookie dough or vanilla ice cream seem like the best choices, but I love mint chocolate chip. And wouldn't Jeni's brown butter almond brittle ice cream be a showstopper?

Allow time for freezing.

TO MAKE THE ICE CREAM CAKE:

1. Crush half the chocolate chip cookies to make crumbs. Combine the crumbs with the melted butter and press into the bottom of a 9-inch springform pan or pie plate. Stand the remaining cookies around the edge of the pan. Freeze for 15 minutes.

2. Meanwhile, soften 1 quart of ice cream of choice on the countertop. After the crust has chilled, spread the softened ice cream over the cake layer. Freeze for 30 minutes.

3. Scoop the remaining ice cream into balls and arrange over the first ice cream layer. Freeze until firm, 4 hours or overnight.

4. While the cake is chilling, and just before serving, make the chocolate ganache.

TO MAKE THE CHOCOLATE GANACHE:

5. Place the chocolate chips in a small heatproof bowl. In a saucepan on medium-low, heat the heavy cream until hot and steaming. Pour the heavy cream on top of the chocolate chips and let set for 1 minute and 30 seconds. Then, using a rubber spatula, stir until the ganache is smooth and silky. Let cool for 5 to 10 minutes.

TO MAKE THE WHIPPED CREAM:

6. In the clean bowl of an electric mixer fitted with a whisk attachment, beat the cold heavy cream, confectioners' sugar, and vanilla on high speed until stiff peaks form.

7. To serve, allow cake to thaw on the counter for 10 minutes, then garnish the cake with ganache, whipped cream, mini chocolate chips, and chocolate chip cookies.

4.

THE FUN STUFF

CHOCOLATE CHIP COOKIE WAFFLES

●●○○○ MAKES: 8 TO 10 WAFFLES

I didn't think there could be anything more comforting than homemade waffles . . . that is, until I created these homemade chocolate chip cookie waffles. The ultimate comfort foods collide! These waffles are delicate with crispy edges and really simple to put together. Chocolate chip cookie waffles are not just for slow Saturday mornings—you can have them on busy weekday mornings too. Make a big batch, let them cool completely, and then store them in the freezer in individual zip-top bags. Just pop each one in the toaster to reheat!

2 cups all-purpose flour

$1/4$ cup light brown sugar, firmly packed

1 teaspoon baking powder

$1/2$ teaspoon baking soda

1 teaspoon salt

6 tablespoons ($3/4$ stick) unsalted butter, melted and slightly cooled, plus more for the waffle iron

1 cup plain Greek yogurt

1 cup milk

4 eggs, room temperature

2 teaspoons vanilla extract

1 cup mini semi-sweet chocolate chips

1. In a large bowl, whisk together the flour, brown sugar, baking powder, baking soda, and salt.

2. In a separate bowl, whisk together the butter, yogurt, milk, eggs, and vanilla.

3. Switch to a rubber spatula and fold the wet ingredients into the dry ingredients. Fold in the chocolate chips. The batter will be lumpy. Do not overmix. Let set while you heat up the waffle iron.

4. Preheat a waffle iron and, using a pastry brush or paper towel, lightly coat with butter. Pour about $1/2$ cup of batter into each waffle iron cavity. Cook the waffles until golden and crisp. Butter the iron in between batches as needed. Serve the waffles immediately as they are ready or keep them warm in a 200-degree oven until ready to serve.

5. Serve with fresh whipped cream, maple syrup, and more chocolate chips.

KATIE'S TIP: You can also use this recipe to make chocolate chip cookie pancakes!

CHOCOLATE CHIP COOKIE TOFFEE

●●○○○ MAKES: APPROXIMATELY 10 SERVINGS

This recipe is derived from a Ritz cracker toffee that I like to make around Christmas. When I decided to make a chocolate chip cookie toffee, I thought *Why not just replace the crackers with cookies in my favorite holiday recipe?* Voilà! Chocolate chip cookie toffee that is super simple to make and a huge crowd pleaser.

14 to 16 regular-size chocolate chip cookies, plus 3 tablespoons cookies, chopped, for topping (the Classic Chocolate Chip Cookie recipe on page 28 is great for this)

1 cup (2 sticks) unsalted butter

1 cup light brown sugar, firmly packed

1/2 teaspoon flaky sea salt, plus more for garnish

1 teaspoon vanilla extract

2 cups semi-sweet chocolate chips

Allow time for freezing.

1. Preheat oven to 350 degrees F and line a 15 x 10 x 1-inch pan with foil. Spray the foil with cooking spray. Place the cookies in a single layer in the pan.

2. In a medium saucepan over medium heat, stir the butter, brown sugar, and salt until the butter is melted. Heat to boiling, then boil 7 to 9 minutes longer, swirling the pan frequently, until light brown in color. Remove from heat. Add the vanilla and stir until blended. Immediately pour this caramel mixture evenly over the cookies in the pan.

3. Bake for 13 to 15 minutes or until bubbly and brown in color. Sprinkle the chocolate chips on top of the hot caramel. Let stand for 5 minutes. Spread the chocolate evenly over the cracker mixture. Sprinkle with cookie bits and a few pinches of sea salt. Place in the freezer to cool completely, about an hour or until the chocolate is set. Break into pieces. Store covered in the freezer up to 2 weeks.

4. Allow to come to room temperature before serving.

KATIE'S TIP: Storing this toffee in the freezer keeps it from getting soft. Bring to room temperature before serving or gifting.

CHOCOLATE CHIP COOKIE BAKLAVA

●●●●○ MAKES: ABOUT 24 BARS

Baklava may seem like an intimidating dessert to make. So many sticky layers can seem daunting. But let me tell you, while this recipe is a little time-consuming, it's not that hard and is 100 percent worth it. A traditional baklava recipe stuffed with chocolate chip cookie dough and then sprinkled with flaky sea salt? Just dreamy.

BAKLAVA

4 eggs, room temperature

1/4 cup sugar

3/4 cup light brown sugar, firmly packed

11/2 cups (3 sticks) unsalted butter, room temperature, plus 1 cup (2 sticks), melted, for brushing

2 teaspoons vanilla extract

1 cup all-purpose flour

2 cups semi-sweet chocolate chips

1 cup shelled pistachios, coarsely chopped

1 cup raw walnuts, coarsely chopped

1 pound of phyllo dough, thawed overnight in the refrigerator if bought frozen

VANILLA HONEY SYRUP

1 cup water

1 cup light brown sugar, firmly packed

2 tablespoons vanilla extract

1/2 cup honey

Flaky sea salt, for garnish

KATIE'S TIP: This baklava gets better with time. Store covered at room temperature for up to one week.

Allow time for soaking the baklava, 6 hours to overnight.

TO MAKE THE BAKLAVA:

1. Preheat oven to 350 degrees F.
2. In the bowl of an electric mixer fitted with a whisk attachment, beat eggs on high speed until foamy. Mix in the sugar and brown sugar until smooth. Add the 3 sticks of room temperature butter and vanilla, then beat until smooth and creamy. Beat in the flour until just incorporated. Remove the bowl from the mixer and stir in the chocolate chips, pistachios, and walnuts.
3. Brush a 9 x 13-inch baking dish with a small amount of the melted butter. Layer 10 pieces of phyllo in the dish, brushing each piece with butter before adding the next. (Keep the remaining dough covered with a damp towel.) Gently spread half of the cookie dough over the phyllo dough. (The layer will be somewhat thin.) Layer 10 pieces of phyllo on top, brushing each with butter before adding the next. Spread with the remaining half of the cookie dough. Add the third and final layer of phyllo dough. Layer 12 pieces of phyllo on top, brushing each with butter before adding the next.
4. Using a sharp knife, score the baklava by cutting all the way into it. Cut along the long side to make even strips, about 11/2 inches wide. Then make diagonal slices, about 11/2 inches apart, to create a diamond pattern. Bake until golden, about 45 minutes to 1 hour.

TO MAKE THE VANILLA HONEY SYRUP:

5. In a medium saucepan, combine the water and brown sugar. Bring the mixture to a boil and then add the vanilla and the honey. Reduce the heat to medium and cook for about 15 minutes. Remove from the heat.
6. Pour the syrup over the warm baklava and let soak for at least 6 hours or overnight. Sprinkle with flaky sea salt just before serving.

CHOCOLATE CHIP COOKIE BANANA PUDDING

●●●○○ MAKES: 8 HALF-PINT (8 OUNCE) MASON JARS OR GLASSES

Banana pudding is about as Southern as it gets. But you know I'm all about classic with a twist. Substituting homemade mini chocolate chip cookies for vanilla wafers adds an extra depth of flavor and texture to an already delicious traditional banana pudding. Plus, these look super cute served up in mason jars or individual glasses.

MINI CHOCOLATE CHIP COOKIES
See page 31 for ingredients

BANANA PUDDING
1 (14-ounce) can sweetened condensed milk
1^1/2 cups ice cold water
1 (3.4-ounce) box instant vanilla pudding mix
3 cups heavy whipping cream
Mini chocolate chip cookies (see recipe on page 31)
4 very ripe bananas, sliced

Allow time for refrigeration.

TO MAKE THE MINI CHOCOLATE CHIP COOKIES:
1. See instructions from page 31.

TO MAKE THE BANANA PUDDING:
2. In the bowl of an electric mixer, beat sweetened condensed milk and water for about a minute. Add the pudding mix and beat for about two more minutes. Transfer to a smaller bowl, cover, and refrigerate for at least 4 hours or overnight, until firm.
3. In the bowl of an electric mixer whip the heavy cream on medium speed until stiff peaks form. With the mixer on low, add in the chilled pudding mixture until just combined and no streaks of pudding are visible.
4. In mason jars or glasses, layer the mini chocolate chip cookies, bananas, and pudding until you have two or three layers in each jar, ending with the pudding. Cover tightly with plastic wrap and refrigerate for at least 30 minutes or overnight before serving. Garnish with more whipped cream and chocolate chip cookies.

KATIE'S TIP: You can also make this recipe in one large dish. I love using a glass trifle dish that shows the layers of cookies, pudding, and whipped cream.

CHOCOLATE CHIP COOKIE BARK

● ○ ○ ○ ○ MAKES: ABOUT 3 DOZEN 3-INCH PIECES

Around the holidays, I jump on the peppermint bark bandwagon along with everyone else. This chocolate chip cookie bark is a play on that favorite, but a year-round treat that you'll never be able to stop thinking about. The butter and brown sugar in this recipe caramelize to create a crispy, chewy bark that is downright addictive. This super-simple recipe is totally customizable. I'm suggesting chocolate chips and pecans here, but have fun playing with your own add-ins. White chocolate chips and crushed candy canes, butterscotch chips and walnuts, or crushed toffee and chopped almonds would be incredible combos.

14 tablespoons (1³/4 sticks)
  unsalted butter
1 cup light brown sugar,
  firmly packed
2 teaspoons pure vanilla extract
1 teaspoon salt
2 cups all-purpose flour
³/4 cup semi-sweet chocolate
  chips, plus more for garnish
³/4 cup coarsely chopped pecans,
  plus more for garnish
Flaky sea salt, for garnish

1. Preheat oven to 350 degrees F.
2. In a large microwave-safe bowl, combine the butter and brown sugar. Microwave in 30-second increments, stirring in between, until the butter is almost completely melted and the sugar has started to dissolve, about 2 minutes. Whisk the mixture until the butter is completely melted. Let cool for 5 minutes.
3. Whisk continuously until the mixture is thickened and smooth and no longer looks separated, about 1 minute. Whisk in the vanilla and salt until combined. Switch to a rubber spatula and add the flour, stirring until no streaks of flour remain. Fold in the chocolate chips and nuts.
4. Dump the dough onto a rimmed 12 x 17-inch baking sheet and pat it into a very thin, even layer with your hands. Sprinkle the top of the dough with extra chocolate chips and nuts and press them down lightly with your hands.
5. Bake until light golden brown and slightly firm to the touch all over, 22 to 25 minutes, rotating the baking sheet when needed. Remove from the oven and let the bark cool completely in the pan on a rack. Sprinkle the warm bark with a few pinches of flaky sea salt.
6. Use a wide, thin spatula to loosen the edges of the brittle. Break into roughly 3-inch pieces. Store in an airtight container at room temperature.

KATIE'S TIP: This bark makes the cutest gift. Add it to cookie boxes with other baked goods or put in a glass jar and tie up with ribbon.

CHOCOLATE CHIP COOKIE CEREAL

●●○○○ MAKES: ABOUT 8 CUPS OF CEREAL

Yes, you can make homemade chocolate chip cookie cereal! And it is *so* much better than the stuff from the box. It is crunchy, not overly sweet, and full of chocolate chip goodness. Eat it anytime of the day with milk, on top of ice cream, or by the handful. The recipe is super simple, but allow some time to roll the dough into tiny balls. It takes about 20 minutes and is a great job for kids because they certainly don't have to be perfect.

1 cup refined coconut oil, melted
$^1/_4$ cup sugar
$^1/_2$ cup light brown sugar, firmly packed
2 teaspoons vanilla extract
2 eggs, room temperature
$1^1/_4$ cups whole wheat flour
1 cup all-purpose flour
2 cups old-fashioned oats
1 teaspoon baking soda
$^1/_2$ teaspoon salt
1 cup mini chocolate chips

1. Preheat oven to 350 degrees F and line a large baking sheet with parchment paper or a silicone baking mat.
2. In a large mixing bowl, using a rubber spatula, stir together the coconut oil, sugar, brown sugar, vanilla, and eggs until well incorporated. Add the whole wheat flour, all-purpose flour, oats, baking soda, and salt and stir until just incorporated. Fold in the chocolate chips.
3. Pinch out small amounts of dough and roll them into pea-sized balls. They do not need to be exact—some can be smaller, some can be larger—but you want to keep them on the small side. Place each onto the prepared baking sheet about $^1/_2$ inch apart. A lot will fit on one baking sheet.
4. Bake for 6 to 8 minutes until cookies are just golden brown. Do not overbake. Remove them from the oven and allow to cool on the baking sheet before transferring them to a cooling rack. Continue to bake the rest of the cookie dough.
5. Store in an airtight container for up to one week.

CHOCOLATE CHIP COOKIE CINNAMON ROLLS

●●●●● MAKES: 12 CINNAMON ROLLS

Every Christmas morning, I make homemade cinnamon rolls for my family, and we snack on them while sitting around the tree opening presents. Years from now, I may not remember what was in those gifts we opened, but I will never forget the way these cinnamon rolls smelled on Christmas morning.

CINNAMON ROLLS

1 cup warm milk

2^1/4 teaspoons active dry yeast

1 tablespoon light brown sugar, firmly packed

4 tablespoons (^{1}/2 stick) salted butter, room temperature

3 eggs, room temperature

3^1/2 to 4 cups all-purpose flour

^{1}/2 teaspoon kosher salt

FILLING

4 eggs, room temperature

^{1}/4 cup sugar

^{3}/4 cup light brown sugar, firmly packed

1^1/2 cups (3 sticks) unsalted butter, room temperature

2 teaspoons vanilla extract

1 cup all-purpose flour

2 cups semi-sweet chocolate chips

ESPRESSO CREAM CHEESE FROSTING

See page 135 for ingredients

KATIE'S TIP: To make ahead, prepare the rolls in the baking dish but don't let the rolls rise at room temperature. Cover and refrigerate overnight. Remove from the refrigerator 30 minutes prior to baking, then bake as directed.

Allow time for rising.

TO MAKE THE CINNAMON ROLLS:

1. In the bowl of a stand mixer fitted with a dough hook, combine the milk, yeast, and brown sugar. Let set 5 to 10 minutes, until bubbly on top. Add the butter, eggs, 3^1/2 cups flour, and salt. Using the dough hook, mix until the flour is completely incorporated, about 4 to 5 minutes. If the dough is still sticky, add the additional ^{1}/2 cup flour, adding more as needed until the dough is smooth to the touch.

2. Cover the bowl with plastic wrap and let set at room temperature for 1 hour or until doubled in size.

TO MAKE THE FILLING:

3. In the bowl of an electric mixer fitted with a whisk attachment, beat the eggs on a high speed until foamy. Beat in the sugar and brown sugar until smooth. Add the room temperature butter and vanilla, then beat until smooth and creamy. Beat in the flour until just incorporated. Remove the bowl from the mixer and stir in chocolate chips.

4. Butter two 8-inch round cake pans or one 9 x 13-inch baking dish.

5. Punch the dough down and roll it out onto a lightly floured surface, creating a large rectangle about 12 x 18-inches. Spread the filling evenly over the dough, using an offset spatula if needed. Starting with the long edge closest to you, roll the dough into a log, keeping it tight as you go. When you reach the edge, pinch along the edge to seal. Using a sharp knife, cut into 12 to 15 rolls. Place the rolls into the prepared baking dish. Cover with plastic wrap and let rise 15 to 20 minutes.

6. Preheat the oven to 350 degrees F. Bake the rolls for 15 to 30 minutes or until golden brown.

TO MAKE THE ESPRESSO CREAM CHEESE FROSTING:

7. See instructions on page 135.

CHOCOLATE CHIP COOKIE CUPS

●●●●● MAKES: ABOUT 18 CUPS

We set these tiny chocolate chip cookie cups filled with milk out for Santa this year, and I have to say that I felt sorry for the house Santa was visiting after ours. To get the cookie dough into the shape of a shot glass, you will need a cookie shot glass pan—easily found online. After baking the dough, coat the inside with melted chocolate to seal the cups so they won't leak milk.

CHOCOLATE CHIP COOKIES
1 cup (2 sticks) butter, room temperature
3/4 cup sugar
1 cup light brown sugar, firmly packed
2 eggs, room temperature
2 teaspoons vanilla extract
4 cups all-purpose flour
1/4 teaspoon baking soda
1 1/4 teaspoons salt
1 cup mini chocolate chips

CHOCOLATE COATING
10 to 12 ounces semi-sweet chocolate chips, melted

Allow time for refrigeration.

TO MAKE THE CHOCOLATE CHIP COOKIES:
1. You will need a cookie shot glass pan for this recipe. Grease the inside of the pan and the inserts. Set aside.
2. In the bowl of an electric mixer fitted with a paddle attachment, cream together the butter, sugar, and brown sugar until light and fluffy. Scrape down the bowl.
3. Mix in the eggs and vanilla, until just combined.
4. In a separate bowl, whisk together the flour, baking soda, and salt.
5. Slowly add the dry ingredients to the butter mixture and mix until just combined, being careful not to overmix. Mix in the mini chocolate chips. The dough will be thick and stiff.
6. Pack balls of cookie dough (about 2 tablespoons in size) into each cup of the shot glass pan. Press the inserts into the center of each mold. Some cookie dough may push up and out of the mold. Leave the inserts in place and scrape the excess cookie dough away.
7. Refrigerate the pan of dough for at least an hour.
8. Preheat oven to 350 degrees F. Remove the pan from the refrigerator and bake for 20 to 25 minutes. Halfway through the baking time, use an oven mitt and push the cake pan down again. Cookie dough will expand out of the mold as it bakes, but you can remove the excess later.
9. Remove from the oven when the cookie dough crust is nice and golden brown. Let cool for a few minutes, then carefully scrape away the excess cookie dough that expanded out of the mold while baking. Let cool completely before removing the pan inserts. Once the crust is cool, twist the inserts and carefully lift them out of the mold. Next, twist the cookie cups and lift them out of the mold. Continue to bake the rest of the cookie dough.

TO MAKE THE CHOCOLATE COATING:
10. Turn the cookie shots upside down and dip the tops of them into the chocolate, then set them aside until the chocolate is completely set. Store in an airtight container until ready to serve. Serve by filling each glass with cold milk and a straw.

CHOCOLATE CHIP COOKIE DOUGH FUDGE

●●●○○ MAKES: ABOUT 16 PIECES

Does anything scream the holidays more than fudge? Christmas tins of homemade fudge passing between neighbors gives me all the feels. This chocolate chip cookie dough version is super sweet, creamy, and soft—the perfect addition to any holiday gifting cookie box.

FUDGE BASE
1/3 cup light brown sugar, firmly packed
1/3 cup unsalted butter
Pinch of salt
1/3 cup half-and-half
1 teaspoon vanilla extract
5 cups confectioners' sugar
1/4 cup mini semi-sweet chocolate chips, for topping

COOKIE DOUGH
1/3 cup unsalted butter, room temperature
1/4 cup sugar
1/4 cup light brown sugar, firmly packed
1/2 teaspoon vanilla extract
1/8 teaspoon salt
2 tablespoons half-and-half
1/2 cup all-purpose flour
1/2 cup mini semi-sweet chocolate chips

KATIE'S TIP: Make sure the base is completely cool before adding the cookie dough. If it is even the slightest bit warm, it will melt the cookie dough and chocolate chips. Trust me, it's a mess.

Allow time for refrigeration.

1. Line an 8 x 8-inch or 9 x 9-inch square baking pan with aluminum foil and set aside.

TO MAKE THE FUDGE BASE:
2. In a medium saucepan, combine the brown sugar, butter, salt, and half-and-half. Stir over medium-low heat until the butter is melted and the brown sugar is dissolved. The mixture should be smooth and combined. Remove from heat and stir in the vanilla. Gradually stir in the confectioners' sugar, 1 cup at a time, until the mixture is smooth and very thick.
3. Remove from the stove and carefully pour the mixture into a large bowl. Let cool completely. While the base is cooling, make the cookie dough.

TO MAKE THE COOKIE DOUGH:
4. In a stand mixer fitted with a whisk attachment, beat the butter, sugar, and brown sugar on a medium speed until light and fluffy. Add the vanilla, salt, and half-and-half and mix until combined. Add the flour and mix until just combined. Do not overmix. Fold in 1/2 cup of chocolate chips. Set aside.
5. The base must be completely cool before adding the cookie dough. Add the cookie dough to the fudge base and stir to combine. Spread the fudge into the prepared baking pan and press into an even layer. Sprinkle the remaining 1/4 cup chocolate chips on top of the fudge and lightly press them into the batter. Chill until set, about 3 to 4 hours, before cutting into pieces. The fudge can be made ahead and stored, covered, in the refrigerator for up to a week.

CHOCOLATE CHIP COOKIE DOUGH TRUFFLES AND CAKE POPS

●●○○○ MAKES: 36 TO 40 TRUFFLES OR CAKE POPS

These truffles make such a fun and special Valentine's treat. They are simple and fun to make and feel exceptionally special. They are not just cookie dough balls dipped in chocolate—but a creamy cookie dough made with cream cheese, making the perfect, smooth center of a truffle. These can also easily be made into fun cake pops, so I've included both options below!

8 tablespoons (1 stick) butter, melted

8 ounces (1 block) cream cheese, room temperature

1/4 cup sugar

3/4 cup light brown sugar, firmly packed

2 teaspoons vanilla extract

1 1/4 cups all-purpose flour

1/4 teaspoon baking soda

1/4 teaspoon salt

3/4 cup mini chocolate chips

2 cups semi-sweet or white chocolate melting wafers

1 teaspoon coconut oil

Mini chocolate chips for garnish

Sprinkles, optional for cake pops

KATIE'S TIP: Use melting wafers for dipping when using white chocolate. Wafers are made to be easily melted, and you can skip the frustration of white chocolate tempering.

Allow time for refrigeration.

1. In the bowl of an electric mixer fitted with a paddle attachment, cream together butter and cream cheese until well combined. Add the sugar and brown sugar, mixing on medium speed until light and fluffy, about 3 minutes. Scrape down the sides of the bowl and add the vanilla. Mix until just combined. Add the flour, baking soda, and salt all at once and mix until just combined. Stir in the mini chocolate chips.

2. Use a small cookie scoop to scoop the dough onto a small, parchment-lined baking sheet. Roll each ball with your hands to make very smooth, close-to-perfectly round balls. Refrigerate for at least one hour or overnight.

3. Once the cookie dough balls have chilled, prepare the chocolate coating. In a small microwave-safe bowl, melt the chocolate wafers and coconut oil in 30-second increments, stirring in between until just melted.

4. **To make the truffles,** dip the balls one by one in the chocolate. Using a fork, lift each ball from the chocolate to allow the excess to drip off. Place on a waxed paper–lined baking sheet and top with mini chocolate chips. Repeat until you've dipped all the balls in chocolate. Refrigerate until firm, about 15 minutes.

5. **To make the cake pops,** prepare a box or piece of Styrofoam with tiny holes on the surface, and check to be sure that a cake pop stick will fit and be supported once you add your cookie dough.

6. Dip one end of a cake pop stick about 1/2 inch into the melted chocolate, and gently insert it about halfway into a cookie dough ball.

7. Dip the cookie dough end of the stick into your bowl of melted chocolate. Drain off excess chocolate and then immediately add sprinkles, if using. Place the stick into your prepared box or Styrofoam to allow the chocolate to harden before storing or serving. Continue with the rest of the cookie dough. Refrigerate until firm, about 15 minutes.

CHOCOLATE CHIP COOKIE GRAHAM CRACKERS

●●○○○ MAKES: ABOUT 24 GRAHAM CRACKERS

This may be my favorite recipe in the book. I was so excited when I finally completed this one. To literally *dream* about something, sit down to create it, and then to have it turn out so perfectly is incredibly rewarding. I will never forget sitting around a bonfire and serving these chocolate chip cookie graham crackers alongside marshmallows and chocolate for s'mores with my family last fall. They are soft (unlike a traditional graham cracker), and they will make you never want to buy the store-bought version again.

2 cups whole wheat flour

1 cup light brown sugar, firmly packed

3/4 teaspoon cinnamon

1 teaspoon baking soda

3/4 teaspoon salt

7 tablespoons unsalted butter, cold

3 tablespoons whole milk

1/3 cup honey

2 teaspoons vanilla extract

3/4 cup mini semi-sweet chocolate chips

KATIE'S TIP: These graham crackers will soften the longer you store them in an airtight container. If you would like to keep them a little crispier, leave the lid of your container unsealed, allowing air to reach the cookies.

Allow time for refrigeration.

1. In the bowl of a food processor fitted with a blade, mix the flour, brown sugar, cinnamon, baking soda, and salt.
2. Add the butter to the dry ingredients and pulse until the mixture looks like coarse breadcrumbs.
3. In a separate small bowl, whisk together the milk, honey, and vanilla.
4. Add the milk mixture to the food processor and pulse until the dough forms and begins to pull away from the sides of the bowl, about 30 seconds. The dough will be sticky and soft. Remove the blade from the bowl and, using a rubber spatula, fold in the mini chocolate chips.
5. Remove the dough from the bowl and form it into a flat disk and wrap it in plastic wrap. Refrigerate for at least 1 hour or overnight.
6. Preheat oven to 350 degrees F and line two large baking sheets with parchment paper or silicone baking mats.
7. On a well-floured surface, use a rolling pin to roll out the dough to a little more than 1/4 inch thick. Note: keep the surface and your rolling pin dusted with flour to prevent the dough from sticking.
8. Using a pizza cutter, cut the dough into 2 x 5-inch rectangles. Using a knife, score the cookies down the center lengthwise, then in half across. Using a fork, prick the grahams on either side of the scored lines. This will create the classic graham cracker cookie pattern. Gently transfer the cookies to the prepared baking sheet.
9. Bake for 10 to 12 minutes. I like to bake them for 10 minutes so that they are still soft and not crunchy.
10. Store the cooled cookies in an airtight container at room temperature for up to 5 days. Eat as is or use them to make s'mores.

CHOCOLATE CHIP COOKIE GRANOLA

●○○○○ MAKES: ABOUT 4 CUPS OF GRANOLA

I love this recipe because it is totally customizable. Add coconut, cranberries, walnuts, ground ginger, or pumpkin seeds to make it your own. If you're adding dried fruit, be sure to add it at the end so your fruit doesn't burn in the oven. This granola is delicious over yogurt, to top muffins, or on top of ice cream.

2$^1/_2$ cups old-fashioned
    rolled oats
$^1/_2$ cup almonds, chopped
$^1/_2$ cup pecans, chopped
$^1/_4$ cup sunflower seeds
$^1/_4$ cup flaxseed
$^1/_4$ cup light brown sugar,
    firmly packed
1 teaspoon ground cinnamon
$^1/_4$ cup butter
$^1/_2$ cup maple syrup
1 teaspoon vanilla extract
$^1/_4$ teaspoon salt
1 cup dark chocolate chips
Flaky sea salt, for garnish

1. Preheat oven to 350 degrees F and line a large, rimmed baking sheet with parchment paper or a silicone baking mat.
2. In a large bowl, combine the oats, almonds, pecans, sunflower seeds, flaxseed, brown sugar, and cinnamon.
3. In a medium heatproof bowl, melt the butter in the microwave. Whisk in the maple syrup, vanilla, and salt.
4. Pour the butter mixture over the oats mixture and stir until well blended.
5. Pour onto the prepared rimmed baking sheet.
6. Bake for 25 to 30 minutes, stirring every 10 minutes to achieve an even color.
7. Remove from the oven and sprinkle the top with dark chocolate chips. Use a spatula to lightly stir the chocolate into the granola. It will melt a little; that's okay. Then sprinkle the top of the granola with a big pinch of flaky sea salt. Allow the granola to cool completely on the baking sheet before transferring to an airtight container.

CHOCOLATE CHIP COOKIE STUFFED SOFT PRETZELS

●●●●● MAKES: 8 LARGE PRETZELS

Ask me who's playing in the Super Bowl, and I usually can't tell you. Ask me for a detailed menu for said Super Bowl, and these Chocolate Chip Cookie Stuffed Soft Pretzels are at the top of the list. At first glance, this recipe could appear intimidating (rising yeast, stuffing dough, and a baking soda bath), but don't let that deter you. It is a fun project that is worth the effort. Make sure you follow the yeast directions written on the package, though. I like to use a candy thermometer to make sure my water temperature is accurate to guarantee activation.

PRETZEL DOUGH
1 1/2 cups warm water
2 1/4 teaspoons instant yeast (1 packet)
1 tablespoon honey
1/2 cup (1 stick) unsalted butter, melted
1 1/2 teaspoons salt
4 1/2 to 5 cups all-purpose flour
2 tablespoons baking soda (used when boiling the pretzels)
1 egg, beaten (for egg wash before baking pretzels)
Pretzel salt

CHOCOLATE CHIP COOKIE DOUGH
1 cup (2 sticks) salted butter, room temperature
2/3 cup light brown sugar, firmly packed
1/2 cup sugar
2 eggs, room temperature
2 teaspoons vanilla extract
2 1/4 cups all-purpose flour
1 teaspoon baking soda
1/2 teaspoon kosher salt
1 1/2 cups semi-sweet chocolate chips

Allow time for rising.

TO MAKE THE PRETZEL DOUGH:

1. Combine the water and yeast in a large measuring cup, stir, and let set for about 5 minutes until the yeast is activated and bubbly. Transfer to the bowl of a stand mixer with a hook attachment and add the honey. Mix until combined.

2. Add the melted butter, salt, and flour to the mixture and mix on low speed until combined. Increase the speed to medium and continue kneading until the dough is smooth and begins to pull away from the sides of the bowl, about 3 to 4 minutes. If the dough appears too wet, add additional flour, 1 tablespoon at a time. Remove the dough from the bowl, place on a flat surface, and knead into a ball with your hands. Coat a large non-metal bowl with oil, add the dough, and turn to coat with the oil. Cover with a clean towel or plastic wrap and place in a warm spot until the dough doubles in size, about 1 hour.

TO MAKE THE CHOCOLATE CHIP COOKIE DOUGH:

3. In a large mixing bowl, with a rubber spatula, stir together the butter, brown sugar, and sugar until combined. Add the eggs, one at a time, stirring until combined and creamy. Beat in the vanilla. Add the flour, baking soda, and salt, and stir until combined. Stir in the chocolate chips. Refrigerate the dough until the pretzel dough is ready.

4. Preheat the oven to 425 degrees F and line a large baking sheet with parchment paper or a silicone baking mat.

5. Divide the pretzel dough into 8 equal balls and roll each out into a rectangle (about 11 x 3-inches). Spread about 1 1/2 to 2 tablespoons of cookie dough along the length of each piece. Starting with the opposite side, roll the dough up into a log, enclosing the toppings

inside. Pinch the seams together. Very gently roll the dough with your hands to form an even cylinder and fully enclose the filling.

6. To shape into pretzels, take the right side and cross over to the left. Cross right to left again and flip up.

7. Fill a large bowl with warm water and add 2 tablespoons of baking soda. Submerge the pretzels in the water, 2 at a time, for 30 seconds. Remove and transfer to a parchment paper–lined baking sheet, placing 4 pretzels on each baking sheet. Brush the tops with the beaten egg wash and season liberally with pretzel salt. Bake for 15 to 18 minutes or until the pretzels are golden brown.

8. Remove from the oven and allow to cool on the baking sheet before transferring them to a cooling rack. Continue to bake the rest of the pretzel dough.

CHOCOLATE CHIP COOKIE TIRAMISU

●●●●○ MAKES: ENOUGH FOR ABOUT 8 PEOPLE

This tiramisu is layered with chocolate chip cookies instead of ladyfingers. The cookies are a little less sweet than you'll taste in the average recipe but chock-full of dark chocolate and almonds, making them the perfect accompaniment to mascarpone cheese, heavy whipping cream, and freshly brewed espresso. This recipe is most certainly in my top five—not only for this book but for all of the recipes I have ever created! It is perfectly balanced, incredibly decadent, and a memorable showstopper.

ALMOND DARK CHOCOLATE CHUNK COOKIES
Makes about 24 cookies

2 cups all-purpose flour
1/2 teaspoon baking soda
3/4 teaspoon salt
1 cup (2 sticks) unsalted butter, room temperature
3/4 cup sugar
1/4 cup light brown sugar, firmly packed
1 egg, room temperature
1 tablespoon vanilla extract
1 tablespoon water
6 ounces dark chocolate bar, chopped into rough pieces
3/4 cup raw slivered almonds, chopped into rough pieces
Flaky sea salt, for garnish

FILLING

2 cups heavy cream
2 cups (16 ounces) mascarpone
1/4 cup sugar
1 teaspoon vanilla bean paste
2 cups strong brewed espresso, warm (about 6 shots)
20 to 24 Almond Dark Chocolate Chunk Cookies (recipe above)
2 tablespoons unsweetened natural cocoa powder

Allow time for refrigeration.

TO MAKE THE COOKIES:

1. Preheat oven to 350 degrees F and line two large baking sheets with parchment paper or a silicone baking mat.
2. In a medium bowl, whisk together the flour, baking soda, and salt. Set aside.
3. In the bowl of an electric mixer fitted with a paddle attachment, cream together the butter, sugar, and brown sugar on medium speed until light and fluffy, 2 to 3 minutes. Scrape down the bowl.
4. Add the egg, vanilla, and water and mix on low to combine. Add the flour mixture all at once and mix on low speed until combined. Add the chocolate and almonds and mix on low speed until just incorporated.
5. Use a regular cookie scoop to scoop the dough. Place 6 to 8 dough balls onto the prepared baking sheet, spaced 3 inches apart.
6. Bake for 10 to 12 minutes until the edges of the cookies are crisp and the centers look puffy and slightly underdone. Remove from the oven and sprinkle each cookie with flaky sea salt while still hot.
7. Allow them to cool completely on the baking sheet for 3 to 5 minutes before transferring them to a cooling rack. Continue to bake the rest of the cookie dough.

TO MAKE THE TIRAMISU FILLING:

8. In a stand mixer fitted with a whisk attachment, whip the heavy cream on high until stiff peaks form, about 3 minutes. Transfer to a medium bowl.
9. In the clean bowl of a stand mixer fitted with a whisk attachment, combine the mascarpone, sugar, and vanilla bean paste and whip on high speed, scraping down the sides of the bowl as needed, until smooth and creamy, about 1 minute. Add the whipped cream and gently fold with a rubber spatula to combine without deflating the mixture.

10. Pour the espresso into a wide, shallow bowl. Set aside 1 or 2 cookies for garnish. Add 5 or 6 cookies to the espresso and let soak, flipping once, until saturated but not falling apart, 45 to 60 seconds per side. Reserve the espresso. Arrange the soaked cookies on the bottom of an 8-inch baking pan, creating an even layer.

11. Using an offset spatula, spread a third of the mascarpone whipped cream evenly on top of the cookies. Using a small fine-mesh sieve, dust 1 tablespoon of the cocoa powder over the mascarpone whipped cream.

12. Soak 5 or 6 more cookies in the reserved espresso, repeating the layering process until you have three layers of espresso-soaked cookies, cream, and cocoa powder. Crumble the reserved cookies and sprinkle on top of the finished tiramisu. Cover with plastic wrap and refrigerate for at least 2 hours and up to 5 days. Serve chilled.

CHOCOLATE CHIP COOKIE WHOOPIE PIES

●●●●○ MAKES: 16 TO 18 WHOOPIE PIES

In 2014 I photographed a pie book for an Amish author out of Florida. I tested, styled, and photographed over 100 pie recipes in 6 weeks. Among the 100 were several variations of an Amish tradition—the whoopie pie. I had never made a whoopie pie before, but they quickly became my favorite pie from the book. This variation marries the traditional Amish dessert with chocolate chip cookies—a perfect combination held together by a marshmallow fluff buttercream.

CAKES
^{1}/2 cup (1 stick) unsalted butter, softened
^{1}/2 cup sugar
^{1}/2 cup light brown sugar, firmly packed
1 egg, room temperature
1^1/2 teaspoons vanilla
2 cups all-purpose flour
1 teaspoon baking soda
^{1}/2 teaspoon salt
^{3}/4 cup buttermilk
1 cup mini chocolate chips

FILLING
12 tablespoons (1^1/2 sticks) unsalted butter, room temperature
1 cup confectioners' sugar
^{1}/4 teaspoon salt
1 teaspoon vanilla extract
2 cups marshmallow cream (such as Marshmallow Fluff)

TO MAKE THE CAKES:
1. Preheat oven to 350 degrees F and line two large baking sheets with parchment paper or silicone baking mats.
2. In the bowl of an electric mixer fitted with a paddle attachment, cream together the butter, sugar, and brown sugar on medium speed until light and fluffy, about 5 minutes. Beat in the egg and vanilla, scraping down the bowl as needed.
3. In a separate bowl, combine the flour, baking soda, and salt. Reduce the mixer speed to low. Add the dry ingredients to the butter mixture ^{1}/2 cup at a time, alternating with the buttermilk, beginning and ending with the flour. Stir in the chocolate chips by hand or on the lowest mixer speed until just combined.
4. Use a regular cookie scoop to scoop the dough. Place 6 to 8 dough balls onto the prepared baking sheet, spaced about 3 inches apart. You should end up with about 32 dough balls.
5. Bake one sheet at a time at 350 degrees for 9 to 12 minutes. When fully baked, a cake tester will come out clean, but the cakes will still be soft. Allow them to cool on the baking sheet for 3 to 5 minutes before transferring them to a cooling rack. Continue to bake the rest of the cookie dough.

TO MAKE THE FILLING:
6. In the bowl of an electric mixer fitted with a whisk attachment, beat the butter and confectioners' sugar together on medium speed until light and fluffy. Add the salt and vanilla. Add the marshmallow cream and beat until fully combined.
7. To assemble, spread some of the filling onto the flat side of half of the cakes. Place the remaining cakes on top to make a sandwich. Serve immediately or store in an airtight container.

CHOCOLATE CHIP MUFFINS

●●●○○ MAKES: 8 JUMBO MUFFINS

When I first started developing this recipe, I had trouble getting that bakery-style muffin top that is oh-so-picture-perfect. Trial and error led me to a couple of tricks. First, fill your muffin tins all the way to the top with batter. Bake the muffins for 5 minutes at 425 degrees F, then for about 25 minutes at 350 degrees F. The initial high oven temperature lifts the muffin tops up quickly and creates a tall crust. Second, let the batter sit for an hour at room temperature before baking to really let the flour hydrate. I know, what a pain . . . but if you want a perfect muffin top, this is the way to get it!

3 cups all-purpose flour

3 teaspoons baking powder

1/4 teaspoon baking soda

1/2 teaspoon salt

1/3 cup unsalted butter, melted and cooled

1/3 cup vegetable oil

1 cup sugar

2 large eggs, room temperature

1/3 cup sour cream, room temperature

1 cup buttermilk, room temperature

1 teaspoon vanilla extract

1 1/2 cups semi-sweet chocolate chips, plus more for topping muffins

Coarse sugar for sprinkling

Allow time for dough to rest.

1. Line a jumbo 8-count muffin pan with muffin liners. Set aside.
2. In a medium bowl, whisk the flour, baking powder, baking soda, and salt until combined.
3. In a large bowl, whisk the melted butter, oil, sugar, and eggs until combined. Then whisk in the sour cream, buttermilk, and vanilla. The mixture will be pale yellow. Pour the dry ingredients into wet ingredients and fold together with a rubber spatula until completely combined, being careful not to overmix. Fold in the chocolate chips.
4. Divide the batter between muffin cups, filling them all the way to the top. Sprinkle with the coarse sugar and additional chocolate chips. Allow the muffin batter to sit at room temperature for 1 hour before baking. This allows the leveling agents to start activating, giving you higher muffin tops.
5. Preheat oven to 425 degrees F. Bake the muffins at this high temperature for 5 minutes then, without opening the oven door, reduce the oven temperature to 350 degrees F and continue to bake for 25 minutes until the tops are lightly golden brown and centers are set. Stick a toothpick in the center of a muffin to test for doneness. If it comes out clean, the muffins are done.
6. Allow to cool for 10 minutes in pan before serving.

CHOCOLATE CHIP COOKIE BISCOTTI

●●●●○ MAKES: ABOUT 20 BISCOTTI

Stop the presses! Literally. We were in final production of this book when I stopped production to squeeze this recipe in at the last minute. I had an idea for a chocolate chip biscotti, but the recipe couldn't be fussy. Here she is in all her glory—a super-simple recipe for the Italian biscuits where the double baking dries out the dough, giving it that quintessential crunchy biscotti texture. I'm so glad she made it!

$^1/_2$ cup (1 stick) unsalted butter, room temperature

1 cup brown sugar

2 eggs, room temperature

1 teaspoon vanilla extract

$2^1/_2$ cups all-purpose flour

2 teaspoons baking powder

$^1/_2$ teaspoon salt

1 cup mini chocolate chips

1. Preheat oven to 350 degrees F and line a large baking sheet with parchment paper or a silicone baking mat.
2. In the bowl of an electric mixer, fit with the paddle attachment, then beat the butter and brown sugar on medium speed for about a minute.
3. Add the eggs and vanilla and mix until well combined.
4. Add the flour, baking powder, and salt and mix until just combined.
5. Remove the bowl from the mixer and use a rubber spatula to fold in the mini chocolate chips.
6. Shape the dough into two 10 x 2-inch logs and place on the prepared baking sheet.
7. Bake for 22 to 25 minutes. Remove from the oven and allow to cool for 30 minutes.
8. Lower the oven temperature to 300 degrees F.
9. Slice logs into about $^1/_2$-inch slices and place back on the cookie sheet cut side down. Each log will make about 18 to 20 slices. Bake for 15 minutes. Flip the slices over and bake for an additional 15 minutes.
10. Allow biscotti to cool on the baking sheet before removing to a wire rack to cool. Store in an airtight container.

OLD-FASHIONED CHOCOLATE CHIP DONUTS

●●●●● MAKES: 15 DONUTS

Nothing says a slow weekend morning like donuts, especially if they're homemade. This recipe takes all the comfort of an old-fashioned donut and marries it with a chocolate chip cookie—perfect on a cozy morning with nowhere to go.

DONUTS
$4^1/2$ cups cake flour
1 tablespoon baking powder
1 teaspoon salt
3 tablespoons unsalted butter,
    room temperature
1 cup sugar
1 egg yolk, room temperature
1 teaspoon vanilla extract
$1^1/2$ cups full-fat sour cream
1 cup mini chocolate chips,
    plus more for garnish
Vegetable oil for frying,
    as needed

BROWN SUGAR GLAZE
See page 139 for recipe
Mini chocolate chips for garnish

Allow time for refrigeration.

1. Whisk together the cake flour, baking powder, and salt in a bowl. Set aside.
2. Using a stand mixer fitted with a paddle attachment, mix the butter, sugar, and egg yolk on medium-high speed until light and fluffy.
3. Mix in the vanilla and sour cream.
4. Slowly spoon in the dry ingredients on medium-low speed. Be careful not to overwork the dough; this will make your donuts tough. Add the chocolate chips.
5. You might reach a point where the dough gets too thick for the paddle attachment. When this happens, switch to a dough hook and keep mixing until all the dry ingredients are incorporated.
6. Cover the bowl in plastic wrap and refrigerate for 1 hour.
7. Roll out the dough onto a floured surface to a $1/2$ inch thickness. You can use a donut cutter or a biscuit cutter and the bottom of a large piping tip to cut out your donuts. Dip the cutters in some flour before cutting so they don't stick to the dough.
8. Once cut, return the donuts (and holes) to the refrigerator while you heat the oil and prepare the brown sugar glaze.
9. Make the Brown Sugar Glaze from page 139 and set aside.
10. To fry the donuts, pour about 3 to 4 inches of oil in a large, heavy-bottomed pot. Attach a deep fry thermometer and heat to 350 degrees F. Once you reach that temperature, carefully place 3 donuts in the pot using a spider strainer or tongs.
11. The temperature will drop below 350 degrees, which is good. Don't make any adjustments to the heat. Fry the donuts for 1 to 2 minutes on each side, careful not to burn them.
12. Remove them from the oil and place them on a tray lined with paper towels. While they are still warm, drizzle with the brown sugar glaze and garnish with mini chocolate chips (optional).
13. Bring the temperature back up to 350 degrees F before adding your next batch. Serve warm!

CHOCOLATE CHIP COOKIE ICE CREAM SANDWICHES

●●○○○ MAKES: ABOUT 3 DOZEN SANDWICHES

A chocolate chip cookie ice cream sandwich is one of those "well, duh" combinations—how could those two things together ever go wrong? But in reality, they're hard to get just right! Have you ever gotten excited to eat a cookie ice cream sandwich and about cracked a molar? Not fun. But don't worry, I've created just the right recipe where the cookies stay soft and chewy, even after freezing. They're not going to last long in your freezer—I promise.

14 tablespoons (1³/4 sticks)
 unsalted butter
1 cup light brown sugar,
 firmly packed
2 teaspoons pure vanilla extract
1 teaspoon salt
2 cups all-purpose flour
³/4 cup mini semi-sweet chocolate
 chips, plus extra for garnish
1¹/2 quarts vanilla ice cream

Allow time for freezing.

1. Preheat oven to 350 degrees F and line two 8 x 8-inch baking pans with parchment paper.
2. In a large microwave-safe bowl, combine the butter and brown sugar. Microwave in 30-second increments, stirring after each, just until the butter is almost completely melted and the sugar has started to dissolve, about 2 minutes.
3. Whisk the mixture until the butter is completely melted. Let cool for 5 minutes. Whisk continuously until the mixture is thickened and smooth and no longer looks separated, about 1 minute. Whisk in the vanilla and salt until combined. Switch to a rubber spatula and add the flour, stirring until no streaks of flour remain. Fold in the chocolate chips.
4. Divide the dough in half and dump each half onto the prepared baking pans. Pat each into a very thin, even layer with your hands using plastic wrap to cover your hand if the dough gets sticky. Sprinkle the top of the dough with extra chocolate chips and press them down lightly with your hands.
5. Bake both pans until light golden brown and still doughy in the middle, rotating halfway through, about 15 minutes. Remove from the oven and let cool completely in pans on a rack. The dough will look a little underdone—that's okay, you want it to be soft.
6. Once cooled, remove the cookie sheets from the pans. Flip one and return it with its parchment paper back to the pan. Spread the softened ice cream over the top and then top with the other cookie. Freeze until the ice cream has hardened. Remove from the freezer and cut into squares with a large knife. Serve immediately, or store in the freezer.

KATIE'S TIP: These should be stored in an airtight container or sealed bag in the *bottom* of the freezer. They will get too cold and thus too hard if left uncovered or stored in the top of the freezer.

BROWN SUGAR CHOCOLATE CHIP COOKIE DOUGH ICE CREAM WITH SALTED CARAMEL

●●●●○ MAKES: A LITTLE OVER A PINT

Whoa! This is honestly the best ice cream I have ever had. Growing up, we'd make vanilla ice cream as a family on the porch of our lake house, all taking turns to tend to the ice and rock salt, then cover it with an old towel to muffle the roaring noise the motor made to turn the dasher. Back then, my grandfather would make the ice cream base out of a vanilla pudding mix and artificial vanilla that he would call "fru-fru juice" for some unexplained reason. This ice cream has the same nostalgic qualities but with all the remarkable flavors of brown sugar ice cream made with real eggs, edible chocolate chip cookie dough, and homemade caramel mixed in.

BROWN SUGAR ICE CREAM
Ice cubes
1¹/2 cups half-and-half
¹/3 cup light or dark brown sugar, firmly packed
6 egg yolks
¹/4 teaspoon kosher salt
1¹/2 cups heavy cream
¹/3 cup sugar

Allow time for refrigeration and freezing.

Place ice cream maker insert in the freezer for at least 24 hours before making this recipe.

TO MAKE THE BROWN SUGAR ICE CREAM:

1. Place a fine strainer over a medium bowl. Rest the bottom of the medium bowl in a large bowl. Add ice cubes to the large bowl so they reach about halfway up the sides of the medium bowl. Set aside.
2. In a medium-size bowl, whisk together the half-and-half, brown sugar, yolks, and salt. Set aside. In a medium-size pot, over high heat, whisk together the heavy cream and sugar. Turn off the heat just as the cream starts to come to a boil.
3. *Slowly* pour the hot cream into the egg mixture, whisking constantly. This tempers the eggs, allowing them to adjust to the change in temperature without curdling. Pour the mixture back into the original cream pot. Place the custard back on medium heat and stir constantly with a wooden spoon for 3 to 5 minutes until it thickens. To test if the custard is done, drag your finger across the back of the wooden spoon—it's ready when your finger leaves a lingering trail. Pour the mixture through the fine strainer into the medium bowl that's resting in the large bowl. Pour just enough water in with the ice cubes so that the ice water is at least halfway up the side of the bowl filled with the ice cream custard. Leave the bowl over the ice bath until it's cool. Stir every 10 minutes or so. Refrigerate the custard overnight before adding it to the ice cream maker.

Recipe continued on following page.

EDIBLE COOKIE DOUGH

1¾ cups all-purpose flour

½ teaspoon baking soda

½ teaspoon salt

11 tablespoons salted butter, room temperature

¾ cup sugar

¼ cup light brown sugar, firmly packed

¼ cup applesauce

1 teaspoon vanilla extract

1 cup semi-sweet chocolate chips

SALTED CARAMEL SAUCE

1 cup sugar

¼ cup water

¾ cup heavy cream

3½ tablespoons unsalted butter

1 teaspoon gray sea salt, crushed, or kosher salt

Almond toffee for garnish

TO MAKE THE EDIBLE COOKIE DOUGH:

4. In a medium bowl, whisk together the flour, baking soda, and salt. Set aside.

5. In the bowl of an electric mixer fitted with a paddle attachment, cream together the butter, sugar, and brown sugar until incorporated, about 1 minute. Add the applesauce and vanilla, increase the mixer speed to medium-high, and beat until mixture becomes light. Reduce the mixer speed to low; add the dry ingredients and beat just to combine. Add the chocolate chips and mix until just combined.

6. You can use a cookie scoop to form balls or place the dough in an airtight container. Refrigerate for at least 30 minutes before adding to ice cream.

TO MAKE THE SALTED CARAMEL SAUCE:

7. Combine the sugar and water over medium-low heat in a heavy-bottomed saucepan until the sugar dissolves. Increase the heat and bring to a boil, without stirring, swirling the pan if necessary. Boil until the sauce is a deep amber color, about 5 to 6 minutes. Remove the sauce from the heat and carefully whisk in the heavy cream. The mixture will bubble. Stir in the unsalted butter and salt. Transfer the sauce to a dish and cool. Store in the refrigerator until ready to add to the ice cream.

8. Select a dish that you'll store your ice cream in. I like to use a metal loaf pan. Place it in the freezer while the ice cream is churning.

9. Churn in the ice cream maker according to manufacturer's directions. Remove the chilled dish from the freezer. Remove the cookie dough and caramel sauce from the refrigerator. Moving quickly, evenly spread half the ice cream onto the bottom of the dish. Use your fingers to distribute half of the cookie dough all over the top of the ice cream, and then drizzle with caramel sauce (you will not use all of the sauce—save the rest for garnish when serving). Top with the remaining ice cream. Mix in the remaining cookie dough and caramel sauce using the same technique as for the first half. Freeze for a few hours before serving.

COOKIES AND MILK POPSICLES

●○○○○ MAKES: 10 TO 12 POPSICLES

When I'm entertaining, I love to walk out with a tray of homemade popsicles for the kids to grab and enjoy. These Cookies and Milk Popsicles are creamy and cold with a homemade chocolate chip cookie tucked right inside. They melt fast, but don't worry—they'll be gobbled up faster than you can see them melt.

12 chocolate chip cookies
  (like the Classic Chocolate
  Chip Cookies on page 28,
  sliced in half if large)
2 cups heavy cream
1/2 cup sweetened condensed
  milk

Allow time for freezing.

1. In each popsicle mold, add half of a large cookie, or 2 cookies stacked on top of each other if they are small.
2. In a small bowl or a large measuring cup, whisk together the heavy cream and sweetened condensed milk until frothy.
3. Pour the cream-and-milk mixture into each mold over the cookies until each mold is filled to the top. Place the popsicle sticks in the middle, cover, and transfer to the freezer. Freeze until firm, about 6 hours or overnight.
4. Loosen the popsicle under warm running water, if necessary, to release from mold. Enjoy immediately or keep in freezer for up to two weeks.

NO-CHURN CHOCOLATE CHIP COOKIE DOUGH ICE CREAM

●●●○○ MAKES: 1 QUART OF ICE CREAM

Chocolate chip cookie dough ice cream is a treat so good it feels like it should be wrong. This recipe takes it even further with a brown sugar ice cream base that perfectly complements the no-bake, edible chocolate chip cookie dough. Plus, no ice cream machine needed!

EDIBLE COOKIE DOUGH
1/2 cup (1 stick) unsalted butter, melted
1/3 cup sugar
1/2 cup light brown sugar, firmly packed
1/2 teaspoon vanilla extract
1/4 teaspoon salt
1 cup all-purpose flour, heat-treated (see directions on page 21)
3/4 cup mini chocolate chips

ICE CREAM
1 pint (2 cups) heavy whipping cream, chilled
1 cup light brown sugar, firmly packed
1 (14 ounce) can sweetened condensed milk
1 tablespoon vanilla bean paste

Allow time for freezing.

Place a standard-sized loaf pan in the freezer.

TO MAKE THE EDIBLE COOKIE DOUGH:
1. Place the butter in a large bowl and add the sugar and brown sugar. Using a rubber spatula, stir until combined. Add the vanilla, salt, and flour and mix until all the ingredients are combined. Add the chocolate chips and mix to combine. Place the cookie dough in the fridge to cool if desired. Once chilled, the dough should easily crumble into 1/8-inch dough balls. Set the dough aside in the fridge while you make the ice cream.

TO MAKE THE ICE CREAM:
2. Whip the cold heavy whipping cream and brown sugar on high speed until stiff peaks form. Mix in the sweetened condensed milk and vanilla bean paste until just incorporated, being careful not to deflate the whipped cream. Fold in the chocolate chip cookie dough with a rubber spatula.
3. Pour the ice cream into the chilled loaf pan and freeze for at least 4 hours. Before serving, let the ice cream set on the counter 5 to 10 minutes before scooping out portions.

KATIE'S TIP: The secret to this rich treat is softly whipped cream that is folded into the sweet milk base. The main thing to remember is that the whipped cream is what makes this dessert so creamy. The last thing you want to do is knock out all of the air as you combine all of the ingredients.

CHOCOLATE CHIP COOKIE ICE CREAM CONES

●●●●○ MAKES: 14 TO 16 CONES

When I first had the idea for this book, chocolate chip cookie cones were at the top of my list. I initially thought of making them in a waffle iron, like you would for waffle cones, but you would need a very specific waffle iron and the chocolate chips would melt in the iron. So instead I thought *Why not make a chocolate chip cookie into the shape of a cone?* All you need are ice cream cone molds—inexpensive metal cones you can find online.

2¹/3 cups all-purpose flour

1 teaspoon baking soda

1 teaspoon salt

1 cup (2 sticks) butter, softened

²/3 cup sugar

³/4 cup light brown sugar, firmly packed

1¹/2 teaspoons vanilla extract

2 eggs, room temperature

1¹/2 cups mini chocolate chips

1. Preheat oven to 350 degrees F and line a large baking sheet with parchment paper. Each cookie will need its own piece of parchment paper. Cut the parchment paper into approximately 6-inch squares and line 6 of them up side by side to cover a baking sheet (for 6 cookies). They do not have to be perfect.

2. In a small bowl, whisk together the flour, baking soda, and salt. Set aside.

3. In the bowl of an electric mixer fitted with a paddle attachment, cream together the butter, sugar, brown sugar, and vanilla until creamy. Add the eggs and mix until well combined.

4. Add the flour mixture all at once and mix until just combined, scraping down the sides as needed. Add the chocolate chips and mix until just combined.

5. Using a large cookie scoop to scoop the dough, place one cookie dough ball on each of the pre-cut pieces of parchment. Place another small piece of parchment on top of the ball of dough and use the bottom of a glass to flatten the cookie. Remove the top piece of parchment and repeat with the remaining cookie dough balls.

6. Bake for 9 to 12 minutes until the edges are golden. Remove from the oven and allow to cool about 2 minutes before handling. Use the parchment paper to flip a cookie over. Take an ice cream cone mold covered in parchment paper and roll the cookie around it, creating a cone. Leave the cookie cone, seam down, on the parchment with the mold still inserted to cool completely.

7. Once cooled, remove the molds and parchment paper. Store in an airtight container until ready to use.

8. Then serve with scoops of your favorite ice cream.

KATIE'S TIP: You should be able to fit 4 to 6 dough rounds on a baking sheet. Once out of the oven, you want to work quickly. You need the cookies to be cool enough to handle and hold shape, but warm enough to mold around the ice cream cone mold.

CHOCOLATE CHIP COOKIE DOUGH MILKSHAKE

●●○○○ MAKES: ONE OVERSIZED MILKSHAKE

As a kid, occasionally after dinner my brother and I would sit on the counter and help my dad make chocolate milkshakes in a milkshake machine. It had a metal cup that, when pressed just perfectly against a lever, would set off a motor, making a long metal paddle spin. This chocolate chip cookie dough version feels like a throwback to that childhood experience, except this milkshake is piled high with toppings.

COOKIE DOUGH
1/2 cup (1 stick) unsalted butter,
  softened to room temperature
3/4 cup light brown sugar,
  firmly packed
1 teaspoon vanilla extract
1 cup all-purpose flour
1/2 teaspoon salt
1/4 cup milk
3/4 cup mini chocolate chips

MILKSHAKE
3/4 cup whole milk
2 cups (1 pint) vanilla ice cream
1 cup cookie dough
  (recipe above)
Optional assorted toppings:
  whipped cream, cookie dough,
  chocolate chip cookies, and
  mini chocolate chips

TO MAKE THE COOKIE DOUGH:
1. In the bowl of an electric mixer fitted with a paddle attachment, beat the butter on high speed until creamy (about 1 minute). Switch the mixer to medium speed and add the brown sugar. Beat until combined, scraping down the sides and bottom of the bowl as needed. On low speed, add the vanilla, flour, and salt. Beat until everything is mixed; the dough will be thick and heavy. Add the milk and beat on low speed for 30 seconds to mix it in. Then switch to high speed and beat for at least 2 minutes until combined and very creamy. Gently fold in the chocolate chips. Set aside at room temperature until ready to use, or store in an airtight container in the refrigerator for up to 3 days.

TO MAKE THE MILKSHAKE:
2. Mold some cookie dough around the rim of a glass and place the glass in the freezer to harden. In a blender, combine the milk, ice cream, and cookie dough and blend until thick and smooth. Pour the shake into a chilled glass and finish with a dollop of fresh whipped cream and assorted toppings.

5.

HEALTHY(ISH) TREATS

VEGAN CHOCOLATE CHIP COOKIE DOUGH BLIZZARD

●●○○○ MAKES: SERVES 2

This "blizzard" is dairy-free, vegan, and packed with protein. Before you knock it, you should try it! The ice cream is made with frozen bananas, and the cookie dough is made with cashew butter, making it creamy, delicious, and completely guilt-free. Even my kids think this is a fun summer treat!

COOKIE DOUGH

3 tablespoons vegan butter, melted

1/2 cup cashew butter (or almond butter)

1/2 cup light brown sugar, firmly packed

1 teaspoon pure vanilla extract

3/4 cup unbleached flour, heat-treated (see directions on page 21)

1/4 cup dairy-free chocolate chips

ICE CREAM

2 bananas, frozen and cut into chunks

1 scoop natural vegan vanilla protein powder of your choice

1/2 cup almond milk

1 tablespoon natural cashew butter

TO MAKE THE COOKIE DOUGH:

1. Add the butter, cashew butter, brown sugar, and vanilla to a mixing bowl. Use a rubber spatula to combine. Add the flour a little at a time and stir until thick and slightly crumbly. Add the chocolate chips and use your hands to fully incorporate the dough. Store in the refrigerator until ready to use.

TO MAKE THE ICE CREAM:

2. In the bowl of a food processor, combine the frozen bananas, protein powder, almond milk, and cashew butter. Blend on high until smooth. Divide between two glasses and stir in the chocolate chip cookie dough. Top each glass with more cookie dough and serve immediately. You'll have cookie dough left over. Keep it to eat later by storing it in the refrigerator or freezer.

VEGAN CHOCOLATE CHIP COOKIE DOUGH BALLS

●○○○○ MAKES: 14 TO 16 SMALL BALLS

If you have a sweet tooth, like me, you need a little something sweet here and there throughout the day to keep you, well, happy. These super-soft cookie dough bites are always stored in my fridge for a quick, guilt-free indulgence. They are vegan and refined sugar–free made with maple syrup and honey as sweeteners. I like to use my very favorite Honey Mama's chocolate, which is a soft chocolate (available at Whole Foods) that hits all the vegan requirements of this recipe. If you have trouble finding it, you can sub dark chocolate chips—just know that they will add a little crunch to your dough balls.

1/4 cup coconut oil, melted and cooled
1/4 cup real maple syrup
1/4 cup honey
1 teaspoon vanilla extract
1/2 teaspoon baking soda
1/4 teaspoon salt
1 1/3 cups all-purpose flour
2.5 ounces (1 bar) dairy-free chocolate (such as Honey Mama's Chocolate), chopped

1. In a medium bowl, whisk together the coconut oil, maple syrup, honey, and vanilla. Switch to a rubber spatula and stir in the baking soda, salt, and flour until well combined.
2. Mix in the chopped chocolate.
3. Use a small cookie scoop to scoop the dough and roll it with your hands into tight, smooth balls.
4. Place in an airtight container and store in the refrigerator.

24-HOUR VEGAN CHOCOLATE CHIP COOKIES

●●○○○ MAKES: ABOUT 16 COOKIES

These dairy-free, egg-free, chocolate chip cookies may surprise you. Even the most discerning palate may not miss the butter and eggs. The key to making them undiscoverably vegan? Refrigerate the dough for at least 24 hours. I am telling you, they are totally worth the wait! The refrigeration allows the gluten in the flour time to hydrate, creating a super soft, chewy—dare I say—buttery cookie that is CCC perfection.

2 cups all-purpose flour

1 teaspoon baking powder

3/4 teaspoon baking soda

1/2 teaspoon salt

3/4 cup dark dairy-free chocolate chips

1/2 cup sugar

1/2 cup light or dark brown sugar, firmly packed

1/2 cup, plus 1 tablespoon canola oil

1/4 cup, plus 1 tablespoon water

Flaky sea salt, for garnish

Allow time for refrigeration.

1. In a large bowl, whisk together the flour, baking powder, baking soda, and salt. Add the chocolate chips and toss to coat. Set aside.

2. In a separate large bowl, whisk the sugar, brown sugar, canola oil, and water briskly until smooth and well incorporated, about 2 minutes.

3. Using a rubber spatula, add the flour mixture to the sugar mixture, and stir until just combined, being careful not to overmix.

4. Cover and refrigerate the dough for at least 24 hours.

5. Preheat oven to 350 degrees F and line a large baking sheet with parchment paper or a silicone baking mat.

6. Remove the dough from the refrigerator and use a regular cookie scoop to scoop the dough. Place 8 dough balls onto the prepared baking sheet, spaced an inch or two apart.

7. Sprinkle the balls of dough with coarse-grained sea salt and bake for 12 to 13 minutes, or until the edges are just golden. Do not overbake.

8. Remove the cookies from the oven and allow them to cool on the baking sheet before transferring to a cooling rack. Continue to bake the rest of the cookie dough.

GLUTEN-FREE CHOCOLATE CHIP COOKIES WITH ALMOND FLOUR

●●●○○ MAKES: 8 TO 10 LARGE COOKIES

When I was researching gluten-free chocolate chip cookie recipes, I found two avenues. One used gluten-free flour and the other used a flour alternative. I decided to include a recipe for each in this book because they have such incredibly different textures—and both are delicious. The gluten-free cookies with gluten-free flour (see page 215) are closer to a "traditional" chocolate chip cookie in taste and texture. The gluten-free cookies with almond flour (like this recipe) are thinner, crispier, and chewier than their counterparts. They have a more unique texture from the grain of the almond flour that I absolutely adore.

2³/4 cups finely ground almond flour

¹/2 teaspoon baking soda

³/4 teaspoon salt

10 tablespoons (1¹/4 sticks) unsalted butter, room temperature

¹/2 cup sugar

¹/2 cup light brown sugar, firmly packed

1¹/2 teaspoons vanilla extract

1 egg, room temperature

1 cup bittersweet chocolate, chopped

Flaky sea salt, for garnish

1. Preheat oven to 350 degrees F and line two large baking sheets with parchment paper.
2. In a medium bowl, whisk together the almond flour, baking soda, and salt. Set aside.
3. In the bowl of an electric mixer fitted with a paddle attachment, cream together the butter, sugar, and brown sugar on medium speed until it's very light, about 3 or 4 minutes.
4. Mix in the vanilla and egg until smooth, scraping down the bowl as needed. Add the dry ingredients all at once and mix on low until just combined. Remove the bowl from the mixer and use a rubber spatula to fold in the chocolate.
5. Use a large cookie scoop to scoop the cookie dough. Place 4 or 5 dough balls onto the prepared baking sheets, spaced about 3 inches apart. Gently press the cookies down with your fingers until about ¹/2 inch thick.
6. Bake for 16 to 18 minutes until lightly golden around the edges and puffed or doughy in the center.
7. Remove the cookies from the oven, sprinkle the tops with a pinch of flaky sea salt, and allow them to cool on the baking sheet before transferring them to a cooling rack. Continue to bake the rest of the cookie dough.

GLUTEN-FREE CHOCOLATE CHIP COOKIES WITH GLUTEN-FREE FLOUR

●●●○○ MAKES: 10 TO 12 COOKIES

One of my top requests when working on this book was to make a really *good* gluten-free chocolate chip cookie. Apparently, there are a lot of bad ones out there! These are *so* good that you won't even be able to tell they are gluten-free. They are soft and chewy and loaded with chocolate. One important factor in the recipe is to chill the cookie dough. This allows time for the dry ingredients to absorb the wet ingredients, which guarantees your cookies will spread more evenly when baking. Also make sure your gluten-free flour contains xanthan gum so it's a 1-to-1 baking flour.

1 cup plus 1 tablespoon gluten-free flour with xanthan gum

1/2 cup oat flour

1/4 teaspoon baking soda

1/4 teaspoon salt

1/2 cup (1 stick) unsalted butter, melted

1/2 cup sugar

1/2 cup light brown sugar, firmly packed

1 teaspoon vanilla bean paste (or 2 teaspoons vanilla extract)

1 egg plus 1 egg yolk, room temperature

1/2 cup bittersweet chocolate, chopped

1 cup semi-sweet chocolate chips

Flaky sea salt, for garnish

Allow time for refrigeration.

1. In a large bowl, whisk together the flours, baking soda, and salt. Set aside.
2. In the bowl of an electric mixer fitted with the paddle attachment, cream together the melted butter, sugar, and brown sugar until it turns into a paste-like consistency.
3. Mix in the vanilla, egg, and yolk until smooth, scraping down the bowl as needed. Add the dry ingredients all at once and mix until just combined. Remove the bowl from the mixer and use a rubber spatula to fold in the chocolate.
4. Use a large cookie scoop to scoop the cookie dough side by side on a small tray lined with waxed paper. You should have 10 to 12 cookies. Place them in the fridge for at least 2 hours (do not skip this step).
5. Preheat oven to 350 degrees F and line a large baking sheet with parchment paper.
6. Remove the dough from the refrigerator and place 5 or 6 dough balls onto the prepared baking sheet, spaced an inch or two apart.
7. Bake for 10 to 12 minutes until lightly golden around the edges and puffed or doughy in the center.
8. Remove from the oven and use a large round biscuit cutter to push in the sides of the cookies, making them perfectly round. Work fast because, as the cookies cool, the sides will firm up, which makes it much more difficult to round out your cookies. Sprinkle the tops with a pinch of flaky sea salt and allow the cookies to cool on the baking sheet before transferring them to a cooling rack. Continue to bake the rest of the cookie dough.

PALEO CHOCOLATE CHIP COOKIES

●●○○○ MAKES: 14 TO 16 COOKIES

These paleo cookies are some of my very favorite in this book. They pack some serious flavor with a base of almond butter and are just sweet enough using all-natural sweeteners. You will need to refrigerate the dough for about 30 minutes to let the coconut oil firm up before baking, but other than that, they are wonderfully simple and quick to make.

1/2 cup almond butter

1/4 cup maple syrup

1/4 cup coconut sugar

1/4 cup coconut oil, melted and cooled

1 teaspoon vanilla extract

1/2 cup plus 2 tablespoons almond flour

1/4 cup cassava flour

1/2 teaspoon baking soda

1/2 teaspoon salt

1/2 cup sugar-free, dairy-free chocolate chips

Allow time for refrigeration.

1. Preheat oven to 350 degrees F and line a large baking sheet with parchment paper or a silicone baking mat.
2. In a medium bowl, whisk together the almond butter, maple syrup, coconut sugar, coconut oil, and vanilla.
3. Switch to a rubber spatula. Add the almond flour, cassava flour, baking soda, and salt and stir until combined.
4. Fold in the chocolate chips (saving a few for on top).
5. Refrigerate the dough for at least 30 minutes.
6. Remove the dough from the refrigerator and use a regular cookie scoop to scoop the dough. Place 7 to 8 dough balls onto the prepared baking sheet, spaced an inch or two apart. Top each with a few extra chocolate chips. Use the bottom of a glass to press down each cookie dough ball to lightly flatten (as the cookies won't spread much in the oven).
7. Bake for 12 to 14 minutes or until the edges are just slightly brown. Remove from the oven and allow to cool on the baking sheet before transferring them to a cooling rack. Continue to bake the rest of the cookie dough.

KATIE'S TIP: I searched long and hard for a sugar substitute that I actually liked. Coconut sugar is by far my favorite; plus, it is better for diabetics and the gut than your normal, everyday sugar, and it holds trace amounts of vitamins and minerals. HU makes my favorite sugar-free chocolate chips. They are sweetened with natural dates (instead of refined sugar) making them not only keto but also vegan and paleo.

GHEE CHOCOLATE CHIP COOKIES

●○○○○ MAKES: 16 TO 18 COOKIES

I loved the idea of creating a cookie with ghee butter because it is a pantry staple and always lives at room temperature. It also adds a beautifully nutty flavor with a buttery finish. The high burning point of ghee makes these cookies crisp on the outside and soft and chewy on the inside. Plus, it is a great option for those with a lactose intolerance; because the milk solids in ghee have been removed, it has very low levels of lactose.

2 cups all-purpose flour
1 teaspoon baking soda
1/2 teaspoon salt
1 cup ghee, room temperature
1/3 cup sugar
2/3 cup light brown sugar,
   firmly packed
1 egg, room temperature
2 teaspoons vanilla extract
6 ounces semi-sweet chocolate
   wafers, chopped

1. Preheat oven to 350 degrees F and line a large baking sheet with parchment paper or a silicone baking mat.
2. In a small bowl, whisk the flour, baking soda, and salt.
3. In a medium to large bowl, use a rubber spatula to cream the ghee, sugar, and brown sugar together. Add the egg and vanilla and beat until mixed well. Add half the flour mixture and mix until just combined. Add the rest and mix until just combined.
4. Add the chocolate and mix until just incorporated.
5. Use a regular cookie scoop to scoop the dough. Place 8 or 9 dough balls onto the prepared baking sheet, spaced an inch or two apart.
6. Bake for 9 to 10 minutes until the edges of the cookies are crisp and the centers look puffy and slightly underdone. Remove from the oven while still warm. Use a round cookie cutter or glass to round out the edges of each cookie, pushing the edges in a circular motion to create a perfectly round cookie.
7. Allow the cookies to cool on the baking sheet before transferring them to a cooling rack. Continue to bake the rest of the cookie dough.

KATIE'S TIP: Ghee is butter that has been clarified to remove its milk solids and water content, leaving a composition that's 99 to 100 percent pure fat. What does this mean when you include it in a cookie? These cookies tend to be a drier, crispier, denser variation of cookies made with regular butter.

WHOLE WHEAT DARK CHOCOLATE CHIP COOKIES

●●○○○ MAKES: ABOUT 14 TO 16 COOKIES

When I was in the process of creating the healthy section of this book, I played with different types of flour, and whole wheat was at the top of my list. I was blown away by the incredible texture and flavor the whole wheat flour added to these chocolate chip cookies. It brings a nutty taste while providing a substantial base for thick, chewy cookies with soft centers and chunks of chocolate.

3 cups whole wheat flour

1 teaspoon baking powder

1¹/2 teaspoons baking soda

1¹/2 teaspoons kosher salt

1 cup (2 sticks) salted butter, cold, cut into ¹/2-inch pieces

1 cup sugar

1 cup dark brown sugar, firmly packed

2 eggs, room temperature

2 teaspoons vanilla extract

8 ounces bittersweet chocolate, roughly chopped

1. Preheat oven to 350 degrees F and line a large baking sheet with parchment paper or a silicone baking mat.

2. In a medium bowl, whisk together the flour, baking powder, baking soda, and salt.

3. In the bowl of an electric mixer fitted with a paddle attachment, beat together the butter, sugar, and brown sugar on low speed until just blended, about 2 minutes.

4. Scrape down the sides and bottom of the bowl and beat in the eggs, one at a time, until combined. Mix in the vanilla. Add the flour mixture to the bowl all at once and blend on low speed until the flour is barely combined, being careful not to overmix.

5. Scrape down the sides of the bowl and add the chocolate all at once to the dough. Mix on low speed until the chocolate is evenly combined. You may need to remove the bowl from the mixture and use your hands to fully incorporate all the ingredients.

6. Use a large cookie scoop to scoop the dough. Place 7 to 8 dough balls onto the prepared baking sheet, spaced about 3 inches apart.

7. Bake for 16 to 20 minutes until the edges of the cookies are crisp and the centers look puffy and slightly underdone. Remove from the oven and allow to cool on the baking sheet before transferring them to a cooling rack. Continue to bake the rest of the cookie dough.

TAHINI CHOCOLATE CHIP COOKIES

●●○○○ MAKES: ABOUT 24 COOKIES

When researching vegan cookie recipes, tahini-based cookies intrigued me. When I started working with it, I found the sesame paste really added a caramel-nutty flavor like nothing I had worked with. It's an interesting flavor that you can't quite put your finger on. These super soft dark chocolate chip cookies are well balanced and sure to be your new favorite vegan baking obsession.

1/2 cup refined coconut oil,
  room temperature
1/2 cup tahini
1/2 cup sugar
1/3 cup light brown sugar,
  firmly packed
1/4 cup almond milk
1 teaspoon vanilla extract
1 1/4 cups all-purpose flour
2 tablespoons cornstarch
1 teaspoon salt
1/2 teaspoon baking powder
1/2 teaspoon baking soda
1 3/4 cups dark dairy-free
  chocolate, chopped
Flaky sea salt, for garnish

Allow time for refrigeration.

1. In the bowl of an electric mixer fitted with a paddle attachment, mix the coconut oil, tahini, sugar, and brown sugar on medium speed for about 3 minutes, until smooth and creamy. Add the almond milk and vanilla and mix another minute to combine.

2. In a separate mixing bowl, whisk together the flour, cornstarch, salt, baking powder, and baking soda to combine. Add the dry ingredients to the creamed oil-and-sugar mixture and mix on low speed until just incorporated. Remove the bowl from the mixer and use a rubber spatula to fold in the chopped chocolate.

3. Refrigerate the dough for at least 30 minutes while the oven preheats.

4. Preheat the oven to 350 degrees F and line two baking sheets with parchment paper or a silicone baking mat.

5. Use a regular cookie scoop to scoop dough balls. Place the balls on the baking sheets about 3 inches apart.

6. Bake the cookies, one sheet at a time, for 12 to 13 minutes or until the edges are just barely golden and the center is a shade lighter.

7. Remove from oven and immediately sprinkle some flaky salt on top of the cookies. Let cool on the baking sheet. Bake the remaining cookie dough.

KATIE'S TIP: Tahini is a paste made from hulled sesame seeds. Choose a lighter-colored tahini and avoid ones with excessive oil separation in the jar, which could indicate an oilier seed type—or it could mean the tahini is on the older side.

CHOCOLATE CHIP COOKIE DOUGH ENERGY BITES

●●○○○ MAKES: ABOUT 20 BITES

Gone are the days when eating healthy meant eating bland—or worse, eating no dessert. These chocolate chip cookie dough energy bites satisfy any sweet tooth while keeping you on track, energized, and ready to go—maybe ready to go make some cookies. But you do you.

1/2 cup semi-sweet dairy-free
  mini chocolate chips
1 1/2 cups (about 7 ounces)
  raw cashews
1 1/2 cups (about 22) pitted
  Medjool dates
1/2 teaspoon vanilla extract
1/4 teaspoon baking soda
1/2 teaspoon sea salt
1 tablespoon vegan butter

Allow time for refrigeration.

1. Roughly chop the chocolate chips into smaller pieces. Set aside.
2. Combine the cashews and dates in a food processor and process until they form a sticky crumble, approximately 1 minute. Add the vanilla, baking soda, sea salt, and butter. Pulse until mixture becomes even chunkier and sticks together when pressed, approximately 30 seconds.
3. Add the mixture to a large mixing bowl and use clean hands to mix in the chocolate chips.
4. Using a regular cookie scoop, scoop out roughly 1-inch balls and shape with your hands. Place in the refrigerator for 1 hour to firm up, then store sealed in the refrigerator for up to one week.

PROTEIN CHOCOLATE CHIP COOKIE DOUGH BARS

●●○○○ MAKES: 10 TO 12 BARS

These cookie dough bars are packed with protein, making them a healthy treat that will keep you satisfied for hours. The first ingredient is chickpeas. I know, I know . . . it sounds strange, but I promise you won't even be able to tell it's there.

1 (15 ounce) can chickpeas, drained and rinsed
1/2 cup peanut butter
1/3 cup honey
1/4 cup almond flour
1/4 cup protein powder of choice
1/2 teaspoon baking powder
1/4 teaspoon salt
3/4 cup semi-sweet dairy-free chocolate chips, divided
Flaky sea salt, for garnish

1. Preheat oven to 350 degrees F and line a loaf pan with parchment paper.
2. In the bowl of a food processor fitted with a blade attachment, combine the chickpeas, peanut butter, honey, almond flour, protein powder, baking powder, and salt. Pulse until smooth. Remove the bowl from the food processor and remove the blade. Use a rubber spatula to fold in 1/2 cup of chocolate chips.
3. Dump the dough into the prepared loaf pan and use your hands to press it to the sides into an even layer. Top with the remaining 1/4 cup of chocolate chips.
4. Bake for 16 to 18 minutes until golden and set. Top with flaky sea salt and allow to cool completely in the pan before using the parchment paper to lift the bars from the pan and slice into squares.

KATIE'S TIP: Chickpeas are a great source of plant-based protein: a 1 cup serving provides about 14.5 grams of protein, almost one-third of an adult's daily protein needs.

VEGAN CHOCOLATE CHIP COOKIE IN A MUG

●●○○○ MAKES: 1 SERVING

When I started testing vegan cookie mug recipes, I made this one and immediately set it aside as a failure when it came out of the oven. It was so ugly—a grainy brown cake that sank in the middle. Later, I grabbed a spoon and skeptically tried a bite. To my surprise I *loved* it. It was nutty in flavor, full of melty chocolate, super soft, and incredibly satisfying. She may be the ugly duckling of the book, but she sure makes the cut.

1 teaspoon ground flaxseed
   mixed with 1 tablespoon water
1¹/₂ tablespoons coconut oil,
   melted and cooled
2 tablespoons brown coconut
   sugar
¹/₄ teaspoon vanilla extract
¹/₄ cup almond flour
1 tablespoon tapioca or
   arrowroot flour
¹/₈ teaspoon baking soda
¹/₈ teaspoon salt
2 tablespoons sugar-free,
   dairy-free chocolate chips,
   plus extra for topping

1. Preheat oven to 350 degrees F and grease an 8-ounce ramekin with coconut oil.
2. Combine the flaxseed meal and water in a small bowl and set aside.
3. In a medium bowl, use a rubber spatula to mix the coconut oil, sugar, and vanilla until smooth. Stir in the prepared flaxseed mixture. Stir in the almond and tapioca flours, baking soda, and salt. Stir in the chocolate chips. Transfer dough to the ramekin, smoothing the top and adding a couple more chocolate chips.
4. Bake in the preheated oven for 12 to 15 minutes or until the top is golden brown and the center is mostly set but still soft. Remove from the oven to a cooling rack and wait until the ramekin is cool enough to handle. Serve warm with vegan ice cream.

APPENDIX

RECIPES TO TRY BY LEVEL OF DIFFICULTY:

This book has something for everyone. From those who are just getting their feet wet in the kitchen, to those who are seasoned baking veterans, here's a list of some of the easiest and most difficult recipes in this book—and a few in between.

EASY

MODERATE

DIFFICULT

FAVORITE RECIPES BY SEASON:

I feel incredibly inspired by the changing seasons. Here's a list of some of my favorite recipes broken down by season, so if you just can't decide where to begin . . . let the current season be your guide!

SPRING

SUMMER

FALL

WINTER

ABOUT THE AUTHOR

Katie Jacobs is a fourth-generation Nashville native author, stylist, and photographer. She is the art director and creator of **StylingMyEveryday.com**, a food and lifestyle blog with a focus on food, entertaining, and DIY. She released her first book, *So Much to Celebrate*, in 2018. She's been featured on the cover of *Southern Living* as well as on the pages of *Martha Stewart Living, Country Living, O The Oprah Magazine*, and *Southern Living Weddings*. She is a content contributor for Reese Witherspoon's lifestyle brand Draper James, Crate&Barrel, and Le Grand Courtâge, among others. You can find her daily on Instagram at **@katiejacobsnashville** or at home with her three kids and husband, creating new recipes and entertaining family and friends.